SUNRISE ON MACKENZIE

DICK TURNER

Published by:

hancock

house

Published by:

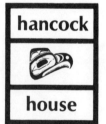

Hancock House Publishers Ltd.
3215 Island View Road
SAANICHTON, B.C. V0S 1M0

Hancock House Publishers Inc.
12008 1st Avenue South
SEATTLE, WA. 98168

CONTENTS

INTRODUCTION 5
1 EARLY DAYS 9
2 OUT OF THE PAST 19
3 BROTHERHOOD 33
4 BERGER HEARINGS 53
5 PIPELINE 63
6 DISRUPTIVE FORCES 69
7 PEOPLE PROBLEMS 81
8 HUNTING AND TRAPPING RIGHTS 89
9 LAND CLAIMS 97
10 SPEECH OF R.D. WARD 109
11 THE JUST SOCIETY 117
12 BROTHERHOOD VIEWS 123
13 ENVIRONMENTAL DAMAGE 137
14 SUMMING-UP 145

INTRODUCTION

Thousands of words have been written about the Canadian North. Most were by authors who live elsewhere, perhaps briefly visiting the great lone land before committing their thoughts and findings to print.

Not so with Dick Turner. He has lived in the Canadian North for nearly half a century, travelling by foot, snowshoe, skidoo, dogteam, canoe and airplane over much of the Mackenzie Valley and Mountains, an area he considers his own backyard. He speaks with a passion about the North, because it has been all things to him for so long, and the people who inhabit the North have been, and are, his friends and companions. It is no superficial relationship, and his thoughts and ideas deserve serious consideration. The words written here, not entirely his own, are the cumulative thoughts and beliefs of many. There is an urgency about this book, a need to get another part of the story available for those Canadians and others interested in this vital subject. This is the year of decision for the North, and the contents of this book should be available to all concerned.

We are all sometimes less than amused by the

workings of Governments. In the North we are surrounded by an ever-increasing bureaucracy, which seems to promote inefficiency and reward the lazy. The largest funds appear to be available for organizations or programs which tend to separate rather than unite. In unity, there is strength, divisiveness brings disarray and weakness. The Government seems bent at times on bringing about disunion and disharmony.

Not everyone will agree with what is written here. Provocative and controversial, the book is written in a style unique to someone deeply involved, someone who wants nothing less than the best for the North and its people. Dick Turner stands to gain nothing in terms of worldly goods, no matter which way the North may go, except perhaps personal satisfaction and peace of mind if things progress in the direction of unity and harmony. He is beholden to no man and is not dependent on others for his well-being.

Read this, and be happy and thankful that freedom of speech is still an important part of our Canadian way of life.

R.D.S. Ward

FOUR NORTHERNERS: Dick & Vera Turner with
Martin & Tina Thomas at Salmon Arm May 1/1977

1

EARLY DAYS

Before the advent of the first explorers and fur traders into the North (including the District of Mackenzie, which we are here concerned with) the native people were strictly nomadic meat and fish eaters. They lived for most of the year in family groups and, out of necessity, travelled extensively. I am told that throughout most of their history they did not even have work-dogs and consequently all their belongings and equipment had to be carried on their backs.

I believe it is almost impossible for most present day Canadians to imagine the conditions under which these people lived, the uncertainties of their lives, their hardships and privations, with the continuous struggle to stay alive with only primitive Stone Age equipment. I am told there were periods of semi-starvation when what little food there was was withheld from the girls and women folk as no more children were wanted at that time and the men must have strength to hunt.

In the Liard and Mackenzie area, their clothing was principally made from moose skins, made somewhat pliable at tremendous labour by the women. In extreme cold weather the moose hide clothing was supplemented by rabbit hides. They had no footwear, only moose hide moccasins which wore through very quickly and also meant that their feet must have been wet and cold most of the time.

Their axes of stone were tied to a stick with moose hide thongs. They made stone tips for their spears and arrows. They carried poles and sticks for many miles high into the alpine country in order to build fences to direct the Dall Mountain Sheep into snares made from twisted rawhide or "babiche," as it is still known. Their knives were made from obsidian rock, chipped into slivers and placed into a cracked rib bone. The women did all the sewing of skins and hides with bone needles. Their cooking pots were made from woven spruce root containers, smeared with clay and baked in a fire. Other containers were made from birch bark, sewn with spruce roots. Men who had seen them said their only fish nets were made from shredded willow bark roots, tied into a mesh, which they found were durable for only short periods.

In summer their camps were in the open, and their animal skin shelters were very heavy indeed to carry, especially when wet. A winter dwelling was laboriously constructed in a circular form using upright poles, with a roof covering of animal skins. There was an open fire in the centre with a hole in the roof to emit the smoke.

·It has been said that at times a child was born and a child died in each family every year.

How they survived the vast swarms of mosquitoes and black flies, God alone knows.

Fire was of course a necessity in all seasons. Since matches were unknown, starting any fire was a major undertaking. They might simply have kept a fire going that had been started with lightning. At any rate we do know that they carried fire with them from place to place sometimes by means of a burning branch as a flaming torch, and sometimes with coals kept alive in an earthenware pot. Body lice were ubiquitous and the filth of the dwellings was legendary.

Some self-styled spokesmen for the native people say this was a good life and they have expressed a wish to go back to it. This was the only pattern known at the time to these people, and there is no shame or stigma attached to that method of living. Homo sapiens (called man by some) has emerged from the Stone Age. The shame is for anyone advocating a return to such conditions, and in failing to give credit to those who enabled mankind to emerge from such an existence.

I believe the facts underlying these primitive conditions must be fully understood and appreciated by all concerned in order to contrast it with the change which occurred from the day the first fur traders appeared on the scene.

With Europeans sweeping into the North American continent and with the Machine Age and technology advancing at an accelerating pace, it seems inevitable that Western civilization with its advanced culture must in time envelop all people of this continent, including all peoples of Canada.

The traders brought whiskey and rum. We see the results today in fatal automobile accidents, pain and destruction on our highways. Has anyone the right to withhold automobiles or alcohol from another person or group? Is it indeed feasible or advisable to do this, even if it were possible? Like many other man-made products, alcohol can produce problems, but I find in our short span of life we all face many problems. Each individual must face each hurdle as he encounters it. If I were to get myself head over heels in debt and my family suffers as a consequence, it would hardly be reasonable for me to cry and moan about the modern world's plethora of goods and services, or the banks and financial institutions whose services I abused, and to rebuke them for my plight.

It would be as sensible to blame excessive drinking on the fact that liquor is available.

Fur traders and others in the early days brought diseases which decimated the Northern people. Communicable diseases are in no way a unique phenomenon. People all over the world have been subjected to plagues throughout the ages.

Some spokesmen for the native groups are reticent about the many items of trade goods which came into the hands of Northern people and had a beneficial effect on their lives. The result must surely constitute one of the most speedy revolutions from a primitive to a modern way of living in the whole history of mankind.

Let me list a few of the items first acquired from the fur traders by these nomadic people.

The first in order of importance must have included a reliable flint and steel and, soon after, matches. From having to carry fire from place to place in a heavy earthenware pot, over hills and through the muskeg and windfalls and swamp, the transition to instant fire is noteworthy.

The next item might be guns which, primitive as they were at that time, were a great advance over arrow, spear and rawhide snares.

Then there were steel axes, vital to a woodsman and vastly superior to a stone one.

There were of course knives and needles and scissors and ice chisels. It takes only trifling imagination to see the smiles and laughter and chattering and the happiness as these products were brought into each household.

There were canvas tents and tin stoves, easily transportable, which made nomadic life a comparative comfort and pleasure. What a contrast, say, to a heavy animal-skin tent and an open fire, in a forty-below-zero day.

Soon available at each trading post were such

things as fleece-lined underwear, cotton and wool outer clothing, woolen blankets (which could be washed) and tough-wearing, reliable footwear. There were diapers for the babies, safety pins, cotton and linen thread, yard goods of cotton and woolen fabrics, enabling all members of the family to be dressed in warmth and comfort.

Soon after the turn of the century, other miracles of western culture began to appear in the northern part of Canada. First came help for the aged, the poor, the infirm and the unfortunate in the form of food rations and clothing. Now an old person need not be turned out into the cold, to starve or freeze to death when his or her usefulness is over. We can indulge this compassion precisely because of the advance of our western technology.

Then came another advance in our Canadian society, resulting from pressure from a few Canadians with a marked social conscience. This was Medicare Service which had a slow and painful birth in the 1930s in Canada. Today in our Northland, medical services are available, free to everyone who needs them. The knowledge and expertise of modern medical science is brought to the most remote corners of our land, with the costs borne chiefly by other than Northern Canadians. Aircraft, almost instantly, bring a sick or ailing person to a modern and well-equipped hospital. Lives are saved, suffering and pain have been alleviated and avoided.

Today, radio, television, aircraft, barges and trucks bring us new and sophisticated consumer items from the south.

Perhaps most important of all, we have at last in the Canadian North a democratic form of government where all Canadians, of whatever origin or ancestry, can and do participate on equal terms.

With medical services expanding, Northern population is increasing rapidly. Young people of both sexes, want, and demand, a place in society, where they can contribute their bit and take the good things of life.

The progressive, modern North of today did not arrive overnight. There were growing pains, setbacks, moments of doubt and dissident voices demanding a bigger slice of the pie.

Eight years after Treaty Number Eleven was negotiated and signed at Fort Liard, in the District of Mackenzie, I first knew the Indians of the lower Liard River Valley. At that time they were still nomadic and they roamed the bushland of the low country and the mountain valleys in a true "land-based economy." There were rough bounddaries within which each tribe or group functioned. A group of eight or ten families would hunt and trap in an area of perhaps 100 miles by fifty miles. They moved from place to place as the seasons changed and as the supply of game dictated. Some groups were made up of only two or three families. Dog teams and skin boats were still used as a means of travel then (1930).

Some of the men who described the former conditions of their life to me were Emil Lenoir, Paul Tesso, Big Charlie, Jerome, Boston Jack, Matou and Yohin. Some of these men were old enough at that time to have experienced the late transition of life from the Stone Age. Their accounts of conditions of their former life are interesting.

During the long periods of relative co-existence with the Mountain Sheep Men of the Nahanni, the lowland people had to be continually watchful. At any time the Mountain Men might appear in a raid. They would lie in wait at the top of Flat Mountain, 5,000 feet above the lowlands. They would wait for days on end, looking for a wisp of smoke which would indicate a Slavey Camp in the vast expanse of timbered lowlands. They seemed to have an uncanny sense of the best time and place to attack.

One man told me that, try as the Slaveys would to cover their tracks to some small obscure fish lake, the Mountain Men would find them, raid the camp and carry off women or girls.

A year when moose and rabbits were scarce, the only hope of food was at the mouth of some creek where the ice broke up early and fish nets could be set in the open water. The gill nets of about three or four inch 'mesh' were made by the women. The material used, the bark of the red willow bush or shrub, was shredded and woven or twisted into strings which was then used as modern 'gilling twine' is used today to make nets. The willow bark strings had to be kept wet at all times. If allowed to dry, they would crack and break.

One of the best places for this early spring fishing was at the mouth of a small creek on the Netla River where, unfortunately smoke would be visible from Flat Mountain, twenty miles away.

Open fires were necessary for warmth, for cooking food and as protection from the vast swarms of mosquitoes. In the words of Emil Lenoir, a full-blooded Slavey born in 1899, and a man of exceptional intelligence:

"Those were very hard days for the people. It was then that they sometimes lost children from starvation. They had no guns then, or knives, or matches. They had only spears, snares and willow bark for fish nets. Fish are not good to live on. The people got weak. They were lucky and happy when they killed a moose. Sometimes for a long time there would be no meat. My father said that at one time when he was young that beaver were so scarce that he knew of only two beaver lodges, where there should have been 100 or more."

"How did they sleep when the mosquitoes were thick?" I asked.

"They would build two big fires, and get in

between them. The mosquitoes would be sucked into the flames."

"It must have been tough on babies. What did women do for diapers?"

"They used 'moss bags' as they do today (1930)," Emil replied: "Moss bags are better than diapers anyway. You just throw the used moss away and get more."

"Do you know if the people ever lived at peace with the Mountain Men?"

"Oh, yes. They would often meet to trade moose skins for sheep skins."

The last serious battle between the lowland and the Mountain Men was said to have been at the site of the present village of Fort Liard. The version which I have is from Charlie Cholo, born in 1908 and interpreter for the Northern Traders Company at Fort Liard in 1930. Charlie's account of the battle is from the old people who passed the story on down to him.

Apparently, early one fall, the Slavey people had a large camp of men, women and children at the mouth of the Black River (now the Petitot River). The camp probably had been under surveillance from the Sheep Men for some time, likely from right across the river, half a mile away.

When twenty or thirty men from the Slavey encampment left the camp on a moose hunt for the day, the Sheep Men paddled across the Liard River and attacked the camp. For some reason the men from the camp returned sooner than expected and arrived to witness the last old men and children being put to death. The returning men were armed with spears and were in an ugly mood when they discovered what was going on. The Sheep Men, now outnumbered, tried to escape, but were hunted down and put to death. Some were caught about a mile from camp, on top of the hill on the south side of the Black River. They were speared and thrown over the cliff. The red rocks of the cliff are said to be from the blood from the slaughtered warriors.

Another version of this battle was told to me by Poole Field, a Metis, born in 1897 in Manitoba and who spent the greater part of his life in the Yukon Territory and the Northwest Territories.

Poole Field said the last battle to take place between the Sheep Men and the Slaveys was at the top of the mountain directly west of Fort Liard. The Liard Men saw the smoke from the camp of the Sheep Men, went up the mountain to give battle, and were soundly beaten.

These could have been two different battles, and both accounts could possibly be correct. There is no recorded history.

2

OUT OF THE PAST

During the first years of the present century at a
time when settlers were pushing west, when roads
were being built and industry expanding and oil and
mineral wealth were being exploited, the Northwest
Territories was thought by most Canadians to be a
useless land of perpetual ice and snow.

It was peopled by nomadic bands of Indians and
Eskimos who had recently emerged from the Stone
Age with the coming of fur traders and missionaries.
Scattered settlements on the main waterways and on
the Arctic coast were made up largely of fur traders,
missionaries, R.C.M.P. and agents of the Department of Indian Affairs.

In the boreal forests Indians moved in family
groups, hunting and fishing for food, and year by
year increasing their fur trapping activities to garner
the pelts of marten, beaver, lynx and fox which were
necessary to purchase the comparatively new and
exciting items of trade goods.

Stone axes and bone needles were a thing of the
past and only the old people were aware that guns,
knives and matches had been unknown until the fur
traders came. Besides the Indians in the bush, there
was a scattering of settlers from southern Canada.

These too were engaged in the trapping of wild furs. Other settlers in the summer months cut the vast quantities of cordwood to fuel the Hudson's Bay Company paddle wheeler which made three trips each summer from Fort Smith to Aklavik with trade goods and supplies for settlements along the way.

When the last steamer of the summer disappeared around the bend, headed for Fort Smith and the winter shipyards, the settlements were left pretty much on their own for the next nine months. When the rivers froze in December, mail was brought in by dog team once a month. And from Aklavik, Fort Simpson and Fort Smith messages could be sent to the "Outside" world by C.W. (Continuous Wave Radio) through the Royal Canadian Signal Corps, who operated transmitters at these settlements. When the Hudson's Bay Company trading post at Fort Nelson, in northern British Columbia, was robbed of twenty-nine bales of raw fur in 1936, it took seven days for the news to travel by canoe to Fort Simpson where it was then relayed by Morse Code to Edmonton.

All people in the bush and many in the settlements lived in log cabins, carried their drinking water from the rivers and most were without plumbing or electricity. Canoes, poling boats and scows were the means of travel in summer and in the winter everyone used dog teams and toboggans.

These years were what I term 'The Golden Age' of the North. And I feel that any who experienced this life, looking back on it, will agree. Most of us lived a hard and simple life. In the main we had enough to eat and took the mosquitoes and blackflies of the summer, and the hardships of the winter in our stride. There were few pressures on any of us such as there are today. Time was measured in weeks and years, not hours and minutes, as is the case today. There was time to visit your friends. Supplies were in the main purchased once a year and you did not have to reach in your pocket for money whenever you saw someone, as we do today. Relations between Indians and others were as man to man, with very little racism ever expressed or implied.

In the early years I was conscious of a barely perceptible social distinction that was known to exist in the North at that time. This I believe was a distinction that existed between Settlement Dwellers and Country Dwellers. It seemed that we who lived in the bush, whether we were Indian or 'white', were thought to be a cut below other residents. Our occupation as trappers was, according to a 1935 occupation survey across Canada, held in low repute. A trapper was low man on the totem pole.

We in the bush, however, with our freedom and independence from the wage economy and the need to be self reliant to stay alive, felt ourselves to be slightly superior to those in the settlements.

This separation of people into social stratas is surely a natural phenomenon. In itself it is nothing to be alarmed about. We know that man is *the* social animal. Nothing in the world is more natural than for people to drift into groups of fellow beings with whom they tend to identify and feel comfortable.

There has been some criticism expressed in the North from time to time regarding the social grouping of people in leisure-time gatherings. The word 'cliwue' is used in a derogatory sense and racism is presumed to exist in the grouping of Northerner with fair complexion.

I would suggest that an honest examination of the matter will reveal that the grouping of Northerners is from common interests and does not stem from racial prejudice.

It would seem that some danger arises to the healthfulness of our human societies if we allow the difference in social groupings to expand and grow into prejudice and hostility. It is obvious that this could lead to conflict. It is equally self-evident that we cannot, even within the borders of one country, live as one big happy family, sharing each moment of our lives equally with every other citizen. Somewhere between we must find a road that leads to a workable and progressive human society.

With the end of the war came the search for oil and minerals. The helicopter gave a new dimension to Northern exploration. More tugs and steel barges were in demand to bring seismographic equipment and drilling rigs into the North via our network of river systems.

Spokesmen for other countries were alleged to have said, "Just look at that vast expanse of Canadian Northland, stretching from the 60th parallel right to the Arctic Islands and the North Pole, Canada, how can you justify your claim to that immense area, when it is settled only by a few roving bands of aborigines?"

And we replied, "Just give us a little time. We are on the march into the Northland. We are building airports and roads to beyond the Arctic Circle. We are expanding the settlements into towns and cities; we are expanding our school facilities right into the outermost settlements; we are bringing Medicare to everyone by building hospitals and greatly enlarging the northern medical staff, with the addition of nursing homes in the very small settlements. Telephone lines go right down the Mackenzie Valley to Inuvik and we have plans to build Microwave stations across the North which will eventually make the land lines obsolete and will bring telephone service to almost every village. We are setting up a new capital of the Northwest Territories at Yellowknife, with a greatly enlarged staff in many Federal and Territorial government departments to handle the terrific job of administrating this vast area of more than 3,000,000 square miles. We have set up a Crown Corporation to develop and deliver power to even the smallest villages. The private sector is busily engaged and is being encouraged by government in an ambitious program in search of oil and minerals. We are sparing no effort or expense in bringing primary education to every child in our land. We are setting up vocational facilities and programmes in two or three of the larger northern towns, which will be free to *all* northern residents in order that the young people leaving school can equip themselves to obtain jobs. By far the greater part of the cost of the new programme will be borne by the southern Canadian taxpayers. We have also set up a Federal environmental program for the North to advise on the construction of many northern projects.

There is no easy way out of the difficulties surrounding us. There is, however, a solution which will allow us all, with dignity and humanity, to attain a worthwhile future within our country. The development and progress of the North must be linked to our search for a better and more satisfying life.

Let us now follow the developments of the Canadian North, in particular the Mackenzie Valley of the Northwest Territories, since the days of what I call the Golden Age of the North to try to see where we and our government went wrong. Not to indulge in recrimination, but to find solutions.

From the late 1930s it was evident that our beloved Northland was in for some changes. Aircraft were becoming increasingly common; our beautiful old paddle-wheeler, the "Distributor" was pulled out on the river bank to rot, and her duties were taken over by diesel tugs and steel barges. Then came World War Two, bringing the construction of the Canol Road and pipeline from Norman Wells on the Mackenzie River, to the Yukon and Alaska; the building of the Alaska Highway, and in 1955-56, the construction of the Distant Early Warning Line in the Arctic.

As the North started to buzz with activity, it was obvious to everyone in the Mackenzie District that the Golden Days of our relaxed way of living were over. The world was moving and we had better get moving also if we did not wish to be left behind. Work was available on survey crews, seismograph crews, oil rigs and government programmes in and out of the settlements. Trap lines were being neglected in favour of a more congenial way of life in the wage economy. Transition to a modern industrial society was not to be easy. It was now seen that the old Indian Act was not consistent with the new life in the expanding economy. Indians said, "We are working side by side with other Canadians, we do not like being classed as minors and second class citizens. We want equal rights with other Canadians with the right to consume alcoholic beverages in bars and in our homes."

The rest of us replied, "It is true. They are right. We cannot expect Indians to accept their rightful places in our society with the responsibility entailed if they are denied the same rights and privileges as others."

The liquor laws were changed and Indians were no longer jailed for making and consuming 'home brew'. But the Indian Act in some aspects is still retained, making the status of the Indian in our society uncertain and somewhat ambiguous. I fully understand the view which some take, that our Federal government have some unfulfilled obligations to these people which are yet outstanding. And it would be abrogating these responsibilites to jettison the Indian Act in its entirety at this time.

For one thing, there are outstanding treaties which to my knowledge have not been settled. Whatever the justification there has been in the past for retaining the Indian Act, onrushing events have rendered it obsolete. The longer the view is held that 'natives' need special consideration, the more difficult it will be for all Northerners to settle into an equitable and a stable society.

Retaining the Indian Act puts us in an untenable position. A native Canadian like myself says to the Indians, "It could possibly be true that my ancestors plowed the land and sowed wheat where your ancestors hunted buffalo 200 years ago, treated you as wards of the state, and herded you onto reservations, with your old way of life gone forever. It is certainly true that a long time ago I paddled north and have lived as your neighbour for nearly half a century. I did *not* treat you as a minor. I did not crowd you off your trapline or regard you as a second class citizen. As a matter of fact, the shoe was on the other foot. It was I who was classed as a second class citizen in northern Canada.

Until this day in the North you have had more rights and privileges than I, a fellow Canadian. Your right to make a living was unrestricted and legal. Mine was restricted and illegal. You were subsidized by the Canadian government in regard to receiving (at no cost to you) food, traps, ammunition and fishnets, and in some cases canvas tents. Because of the colour of my skin, none of those things was available to me.

And just for the record, you know as well as I do, a fact which most southerners do not: that up to the present day, Indians in the N.W.T. are given more help in job opportunities, taking of game, government financial help in business, than Canadians of southern origin such as myself.

You and I know that we in the North surmounted hardships which southern Canadians today would say were impossible. Today we have a different set of problems, but which are far easier to overcome than, say, a 100-mile trip by dogteam through deep, wet snow.

I would suggest we all forget 200 years ago. None of us now living can be held accountable for what was done, good or bad. What we do know is that we now have an obligation and a duty to industrialize and expand our economy, so that within the framework of our society all northerners will be able to fulfil the search for a better life.

There are many factors involved in the developing and changing North. First is the Indian population increase which began with the introduction of expanded free medical services in the Northwest Territories. Then came the legality of the consumption of alcohol through government liquor stores and bars throughout the land, and the lowering of the legal age limit.

Starting in the 1950s, many Indians were entering the wage economy as oil exploration began to take place and the road building program got underway. But with so many young people coming into the wage market there were not enough jobs available for all those looking for employment. In many settlements there were very few employment opportunities, especially in the winter months. In most cases a living of sorts could still be made by trapping in winter and early spring. 'Living off the land', it was termed.

In some areas wild game and wild fur was available, but the supply was uncertain. For a variety of very good reasons dogteams were becoming fewer and the use of motor toboggans was becoming very popular. In most of the District of Mackenzie, in the space of two decades, trapping had gone from a traditional winter occupation for all male residents to a part-time almost recreational activity. The Department of Game Management of the N.W.T. is expending much effort and expense in activating programs to encourage young Indian men to get out into the bush in the winter and crop the fur-bearing animals available. Subsidies are offered in one form or another (detailed later in this essay) and loans for traps and supplies are available. The success of these programs is marginal, with the numbers of full-time trappers steadily decreasing.

The view has been expressed in the North that in light of the fact that trapping privileges are mainly restricted to Indians, why is it that so few of them take advantage of the opportunity? When the only alternative for many is to accept welfare, why do not more go to the bush in the winter to hunt and trap? The answer is, first, that a substantial financial outlay is required in this modern age for a trapper to set himself up. Snowmobiles are practical and necessary for winter trapline operation on the endless network of seismograph cutlines in the bush, which criss-cross almost the whole expanse of the Mackenzie and Liard River areas. The work is hard. The life is lonely. The financial returns are uncertain.

Most Northern people live in settlements where there is television and other diversions. If there is any way out, you cannot expect many young men to choose a trapper's way of life.

It follows that in many if not all Northern settlements in the Mackenzie Valley, when jobs are not available, you will find many able-bodied people on welfare. Everyone knows that it is humiliating for an able-bodied man to live for any length of time on welfare. Welfare, I submit, is a manifestation of man's compassion for another and is (or was, at its inception) meant only to relieve the financial stress of a particular situation. The authorities who administer the welfare programmes do not force welfare upon anyone. The applicant must apply for assistance and submit to a certain amount of questioning. In all settlements there are daily expenses which have to be met. The situation becomes controversial in cases where one or more members of a household are gainfully employed and others in the household are accepting welfare. There are cases on record where an able-bodied recipient of welfare has screamed to high heaven when consideration was given to withdrawing the payments.

In light of the facts of the situation, it is inexplicable to me that Indian leaders will curse the 'white man' down for introducing welfare, and couple welfare and booze as being the destructive elements in the largely unfortunate position of some Indians in our society today.

The 'white man' is blamed for introducing alcohol to the Indians and according to some spokesmen the 'white man' is utterly and completely responsible for cases which are all too common, where an Indian is on welfare and spends a good part of his time in the pub or in his home in a drunken condition. They point to the fact that there are more Indians than others on welfare, that most of those picked up on the streets in a drunken condition in the North are Indians, and a high percentage of those in jail are Indians.

They scream with indignation, "Curse your white society and all the degradation you have brought upon us. You have despoiled our land, forced your degenerate culture of greed upon us and taken our old beautiful way of life from us. White Man, go back to the southlands and take your artifice, your corrupt ways and your deceit with you. Leave our gentle people to live in harmony with The Great Spirit, where for thousands of years before your coming we lived an idyllic existence, at peace with one another, the animals and Nature.

"But—hey, wait a minute! Before you go, don't forget to leave us your liquor stores with a good supply of booze, your hospitals and doctors and nurses, your jet aircraft and your hard-surfaced runways, your schools and money to run them. We will supply the teachers ourselves. Then because we have been treated with such injustice, we demand you set up a trust fund (a land rights fund?) for all

Indians in perpetuity, of millions and millions of dollars so that each and every one of us (and our leaders) can live in luxury. We have learned to love such things as radio and television, nicely packaged variety of foods in the stores, warm clothing, shoes and boots, record players, bicycles, fishing rods, cameras and outboard motors. We will need money for these things. Leave also the low rental houses with their oil furnaces. We like them better than our old skin teepees and our circular log houses with an open fire. And leave us the cars and pick-ups, and money and machinery for the upkeep of the roads, for we cannot drive automobiles in the muskegs. We will demand more items later, but that will be enough for now."

I have carefully excluded the many Indians of the Mackenzie Valley from the wild talk of some of the leaders. I believe that many Indian men and women of today are too intelligent and honest to indulge in the verbiage that some of their leaders are using. And the position their southern advisors are taking is at least noteworthy.

The most unreasonable and ridiculous demands made on behalf of the Indians originate from southern Canadians. It seems that in their rejection of some of the undesirable consequences of our western society, and their sympathy for the plight of the Indians, they have with self-righteous anger and indignation been advocating and advising the Indian leaders in demands that at first glance might seem reasonable, but are in effect completely unreasonable and unrealistic. It is another instance where southern do-gooders and bleeding hearts have leaped in with self-assured confidence to right the wrongs of our society and to bring light and direction to a situation of which they know very little. Why is the position they take so diametrically opposed to the general opinion of Northerners? Have they been given some Divine insight into the problems that we as common northern Canadians have not? Are they more politically aware than we? Have they been endowed with a social conscience which we have not? In desperation the accusation is made that we are prejudiced.

In these late years in the North there has developed an attitude or frame of mind among some segments of the population that the newly seen wealth of our modern society can be had on demand. Advisors from southern Canada to the so-called 'native' groups must share part of the responsibility for the erroneous conception that clients can expect a free ride in our society. In a primitive society where all energy is needed to barely maintain life, it is just not possible to stockpile excess supplies. To anyone emerging from a bare existence society to a wealth of goods, it could at first glance appear that you walk up and take what you need. It is a sore blow to some to discover that the rules are essentially the same as before. There are no concessions for those able to paddle their own canoes.

It seems to me that all human beings are programmed to wish to contribute their best efforts for any reward. A prolonged free ride for an individual or a group saps pride and ego, and destroys. Conversely, if they make an effort, and are rewarded for it, then each can stand tall. We are all alike in that we cannot operate without pride and self-respect. *But*—we do not need to live in a mansion, or be in a position of authority to maintain our self-respect. I have lived for many years in small cabins with primitive facilities (with no more income than the Indians of the area), where all items of food, clothing, books and trapline supplies were bought and paid for by our own effort of hand and brain. My neighbours (Metis, Indian and white) lived exactly as I did and felt the same pride as I did.

None of us foresaw that within forty years cries of

'prejudice', 'discrimination', and 'arrogance' would be heard throughout the land. Something of concern to all of us has developed in the North in those intervening years. One misunderstanding that might have contributed to the present dilemma is that centered around the too-well-known word 'welfare'. Welfare itself in the North is used, abused, praised and cursed. Our country offers a helping hand to those citizens who through unfortunate circumstances find themselves in need. The criteria of success in application for assistance is based on *need*. Need of help because of mental or physical defects; need because of advancing age; need of temporary financial assistance when a person finds himself in difficulty through no fault of his own.

In the change-over from a primitive to a modern society, many people of northern ancestry, having difficulty in the transition, applied for and received financial assistance. The government generously responded and now we find a situation where 'welfare' has received an unjustifiably 'native' connotation, which is one of the problems we have in the North today.

3

BROTHERHOOD

The contemplated construction of the Mackenzie Valley pipeline is probably the most important enterprise that has or will ever face Northerners. For it is our big chance to start on the road to development and industrialization. The wealth from natural resources (unrenewable resources), if it is handled right, will give us the time, the money and the expertise to establish renewable resource industries on a permanent basis. With a high degree of employment and with education opportunities expanding and keeping pace with our maturing political institutions, we should be well on the way to solving the economic, cultural and social problems which demand attention.

Now, out of the blue sky comes a cloud which threatens to dump a cold shower upon us and to destroy our future, with controversy and dissension. The disruption centered around the formation of the N.W.T. Indian Brotherhood, claiming to represent the Treaty Indians of the Northwest Territories. Their purpose is said to be the finalizing of land claims, and something they term 'aboriginal' rights. They are taking advantage of every turn in the road, every lever and every tool, to wrest from Canadian society special status and privileges over and above other Canadians. They call themselves 'natives' and seem to assume they have some God-given right to special consideration. If they are 'natives' what does that make me? 'Native' to me is the place of origin of a person or thing, i.e. 'one's native land'. Let us not use as an argument against other citizens the fact that we are native Canadians.

The Brotherhood, egged on by their southern advisors and sympathizers, are opposing the building of the Mackenzie Valley pipeline. This has brought about a confrontation with many other Northerners. An atmosphere of confrontation is the worst possible environment for a reasoned solution.

There never have been Indian Reserves within the N.W.T., nor any attempt to push any ethnic group into a corner or fence them off in any way from our northern society. The Federal government (through the N.W.T. administration) has been more than generous in its concern and financial assistance for *all* northerners in helping them to adjust to modern culture. But equality has apparently not been good enough for the Brotherhood leaders. They want more. What is worse, if they get their way, other Northerners more numerous than the Brotherhood will be denied the opportunity for a better life.

Brotherhood leaders and spokesmen have been quoted over the past few years in news reports, the Berger hearings and in various other sources. Their views, comments, and demands can be summed up as follows:

The Brotherhood is adamantly opposed to the construction of the Mackenzie Valley pipeline until all so-called 'Native Land Claims' have been settled to their satisfaction. They claim jurisdiction over the land where the pipeline will run, and want at least a ten-year moratorium until a start is made on the construction.

They demand the 450,000 square miles of the Mackenzie Valley to set up their own Dene nation.

They demand funds from the government in grants and royalties accruing from any oil and gas development. In short, they claim that the North has always belonged to the Treaty Indians whom they claim to represent and they want complete compensation for anything of value from the resources of the North.

Their opening statement to the Berger Hearings reads:

"It is in the communities of the Mackenzie Valley, Mr. Commissioner, that you will hear most clearly the voice of the Native people—people who are truly of the very land on which they live. The people know that through this Enquiry they will be speaking to all Canadians, and they will speak from their hearts. They will speak of many things, not only of the pipeline, but also of their lives—the good times and the bad times, their hardships and their hopes. But most of all they will speak of their land—the land which sustains their bodies, the land which shapes their society, the land which quickens their souls.

"Why, then, are we here? The answer, Mr. Commissioner, is quite simple. This Enquiry is our one and only chance to examine in detail the pipeline proposal; it is also the best way for us to put before the people of Canada our position on the settlement of the Native land claims in the Northwest Territories. Indeed we give priority to the issues relating to the land claims.

"...was the fact that for the Native people in southern Canada the C.P.R. was a disaster. It meant the loss of their land and the slaughter of the buffalo herd upon which their livelihood depended. It is with a view to avoiding this sort of fate that the Native people of the North will take the position before this Enquiry that there should be no pipeline before a land claim settlement."

From another statement to the Berger Hearings: "By the late 1960s, our dissatisfaction with maltreatment by the government had reached a point that we decided we, like our brothers and sisters in the South, needed a Brotherhood to protect our interests as a people.

"At about the same time the Federal Government issued its infamous White Paper on Indian Affairs, which essentially abolished the special relationship between Treaty Indians in Canada and the Federal Government as set out in the Indian Act. Indian organizations across Canada rejected this paper because it would eliminate the Federal Government's constitutional responsibility to Indian people, and would remove the special status which the Treaties with the Crown gave to Indian nations.

"Then and now, our struggle over Treaty rights was seen as part of the broader struggle to establish aboriginal rights for all people of native ancestry in the N.W.T. ."

From other submissions to the Berger Hearings, "The Dene have suffered from white arrogance since 1789." "The recent history of the Dene is a story of struggle, the struggle of a people for self-determination and against colonial control, for natural survival and against cultural genocide."

. Harold Cardinal is a member of the board of the National Indian Brotherhood, and because of his book, *The Unjust Society*, he must be considered a spokesman for the Indian Brotherhood.

He writes, "The Federal Government policy of June 1969 is a thinly disguised program of extermination through assimilation.

"The native people of Canada look back on generations of accumulated frustration under conditions which can only be described as colonial, brutal and tyrannical.

"I will expose the ignorance and bigotry that has impeded our progress, the eighty years of educational neglect that have hobbled our young for generations, the gutless politicians who have knowingly watched us sink in the quicksands of apathy and despair and have failed to extend a hand.

"We will know they (the Federal Government) have nothing to say. We will know they speak with forked tongue.

"There are precedents for the present government's betrayal; the white man took what we gave him, and more, but we never received payment. It was planned that way.

"Bigotry? The problem grows worse, not better. A survey by the Canadian Corrections Association, reveals some of the problems that the native person faces in the area of prejudice and discrimination.

"We do not want the Indian Act retained because it is a good piece of legislation. It isn't. It is discriminatory from start to finish. But it is a lever in our hands and an embarrassment to the government, as it should be. No just society, and no society with even pretensions to being just, can long tolerate such a piece of legislation, but we would rather continue to live in bondage under the inequitable Indian Act than surrender our sacred rights.

"The young (Indian) generation that is even now flexing its muscles does not have the patience the older leaders have shown.... They will not believe that the present system can work to change our situation. They will organize and organize well. But, driven by frustration and hostility, they will organize not to create a better society, but to destroy your society.

"The present course of the federal government drives the Indian daily closer and closer to the second alternative...despair, hostility, destruction."

Just at the time when the North was emerging from a sort of economic and cultural Ice Age in the early 1960s, and we had reached a land-mark of political democracy with an elected advisory Legislature in the Northwest Territories, and with the administration going all out to help every northerner to attain a degree of independence, pride and economic improvement, many of us saw with alarm the emergence of the N.W.T. Indian Brotherhood with the backing of white advisors from southern Canada. Their object seemed to be to establish a racist organization in the North, and particularly in the District of Mackenzie, to demand a hold-up on progress in the North until they decided just how much they would demand in land claims and aboriginal rights. With the help of southerners and a favourable press and radio coverage, they succeeded in bringing the construction of the Mackenzie Highway to a halt.

At first glance it seems surprising that with the power and support the Brotherhood now had, that a stop was not made in the drilling for oil and gas in the Mackenzie Delta and the Beaufort Sea. The drilling did go ahead and quantities of oil and gas were discovered, with a potential production that seemed to warrant a gas pipeline to the south. With the value of potential oil and gas reserves now mounting into astronomical sums, it became apparent why there was so little opposition by the Brotherhood to the drilling programs. The stakes in the game for ownership of the land were now quite large and well-worth fighting for. The strategy of the advisors to the Brotherhood came to light.

Next they dug in their heels and bucked the development of the Mackenzie Valley Pipeline with every means at their disposal, even threatening violence if they did not get their way. Their verbal attacks bordered at times on the subversive, with threats of violence against crown lands and property.

An organization such as they have does not flourish on muskeg moss, river water and northern air alone. Funding had to come from somewhere. Where did they get the vast sums for legal advice and their stream of propaganda? From our Federal Treasury, it seems. I have it on the highest authority, from officials of the Government of the Northwest Territories, that between 1970 and 1976 the Federal Government gave the Brotherhood and other 'native' organizations a sum in excess of $16,000,000.

Some of the views expressed by Brotherhood officials, their advisors and their spokesmen consistently refer to *all* Crown lands in the District of Mackenzie as *their* land, which seems at the very least to be a doubtful proposition. In Treaty Number Eleven all rights to the land was given over to the Government of the Dominion of Canada.

They speak often of something they call "aboriginal rights" as if this were a Divine right from Heaven. I declare just as vehemently that there is no such thing in Canada as "aboriginal rights" for anyone.

In light of the fact that many young people of the North in the early 1970s were entering the wage market at a time when the ranks of the unemployed were already swollen, most people in the Mackenzie Valley reacted with pleasure and enthusiasm to Prime Minister P.E. Trudeau's announcement that the Mackenzie Highway would be extended from Fort Simpson to Inuvik and at some future date a gas pipeline to southern Canada would be considered. Work was started on the highway and many northerners were employed in clearing the right-of-way. At the same time a large training program was set up 100 miles north of Fort Simpson to train 'natives' in operating and servicing heavy duty road equipment for the actual construction of the highway.

Young men were brought by air at government expense from settlements all over the Northwest Territories to work in the training and clearing camps. I can verify that some of the Indian operators of heavy equipment on that project were peerless in their vocation.

In September of 1973 the N.W.T. Indian Brotherhood, with the help of their southern advisors,
decided to ask Judge Willam Morrow of the
Supreme Court of the Northwest Territories to issue
a caveat to suspend all land transactions pertaining
to Crown land in the Mackenzie Valley until the
Brotherhood had time to build and present a case
against the building of the corridor. Some of us were
surprised to hear the caveat was duly issued. Soon
after this, work on the Mackenzie Highway to
Inuvik came to a halt. Though some construction
continued, the employment of natives was much
reduced.

Apparently many things in Canada have changed
over the past years. Some of the rules of the game
have been summarily altered. I wonder if the C.P.R.
transcontinental railroad, our highways, or the
powerlines across the country would ever have been
built if a handful of dissidents could have had the
courts issue caveats to hold up such developments
until they had demanded and received government
money to marshal their lawyers to establish an
argument to retard development. I suggest if we had
followed that line we still would be plowing our
fields with horses and hoeing our corn by hand.

The Brotherhood says in effect, "This is our land.
With your money we will establish our case and
when we are good and ready we will tell you how
much you will have to pay us in cold cash to have
the privilege of constructing the corridor to the
Arctic to transport *our* gas and oil to the south. We
will tell you how many Indians you must employ on
the construction jobs and we will lay down the
conditions, all the conditions, upon which you will
operate.

To attain their objectives, particularly in their
demand for subsidies, the Indian Brotherhood has
made a variety of attempts via radio, press and
television to persuade southern Canadians who, by

their votes control the purse strings of the Federal government, to allow vast sums of money to flow into their coffers. Lately they have used threats of violence to bolster their demands. In most civilized countries, threats of violence to attain political objectives would be illegal, and would not be tolerated. Our government not only tolerates veiled threats of blowing up the pipeline (if the construction proceeds without acceding to the demands of the Brotherhood), but it continues to hand out large sums of money to an organization which seems to encourage such irresponsible talk.

An assessment of one main tactic used to attain their objectives is reviewed below. It is an old game and it has been used before to gain a point or to shore up a weak position. It is an argument that starts out with statements of truth and facts, gradually blending into half-truths and finally to downright dissembling.

The facts are that for far too long Canadian Indians have been classed as wards of the government, or second class citizens if you prefer, and that treaties made with them many years ago have not been finalized. Then the grey area is approached. This is the claim made for aboriginal rights for all Indians. The word they often use is 'native'. I consider myself to be a native Canadian and feeling that they do not wish to include me in their 'aboriginal' rights claims, I use the word 'Indian' to avoid misunderstanding. Aboriginal rights is in the area of what I term as a half truth, for there are many Canadians including myself who deny citizens of our country any aboriginal rights.

It is claimed that they had a proper regard for the Great Spirit, and lived in harmony with nature. Man, then, had dignity and pride, having compassion for man and animals alike. That, they say, is the right way for man to live and that is the way they would have continued to live if the Europeans had not come along to desecrate the country and demoralize the people with whiskey, beads, government liquor stores, welfare, and the machines to rip up the virgin land right and left. Some Brotherhood spokesmen say, "Give us the Mackenzie Valley as a Dene Nation, (because that is where you want to build the pipeline). Give us all the money we demand, and then we can go back to the good old days and live as we did before you spoiled it all for us."

But then we hear that for a price they will allow us to build the pipeline (after a ten- or fifteen-year waiting period). With the money, what would they do? Would they live in the bush, trapping and hunting, 20,000 Indians? Would they live in animal-skin teepees and be at peace with one another and the animal kingdom?

Some of their spokesmen say if the pipeline is built now it will upset the environment and cause havoc with the animals, especially the caribou. But if the Indians have jurisdiction over building the pipeline, then suddenly it will not bother the caribou or the ecology at all.

Could anyone but an idiot be expected to swallow such utter drivel? They should get together with their assorted advisors and brush up on their propaganda.

The dishonesty of the position taken by the Brotherhood is abundantly apparent. I believe they do not wish to go back to the Stone Age, any more than I do. People throughout the world have always clamoured for the amenities of civilization. Northerners will never willingly give up their comforts for an igloo, a teepee and a stone axe.

Something might be said here as to how democratic the N.W.T. Indian Brotherhood organization is, and to what extent the organization has grass roots support from Indians on the street, or in the bush, as it were. I have implied that the Brotherhood propaganda does not generally reflect the views of the Northern native population. This is especially true of those 'natives' who are classed as Metis.

I feel that the Brotherhood leaders represent no more than a few individuals who have learned to exploit the guilt-ridden southern do-gooders to help the Brotherhood attain Federal subsidies. Payments designed not only to fund their lives but also to fund a host of legal battles aimed at further extending the funding.

Their lamentations and expressions of love for Mother Earth and a return to the old ways, and so forth, though they sound romantic, are totally unrealistic. The white man in this drama is cast as the "bad guy." Is this not the old Cowboy and Indian game in reverse?

It is evident from the position taken by the spokesmen for the Brotherhood that their objective is to paint the most dismal picture possible of the position of the Indians in the North in order to arouse pity in the hearts of southern voters. This is not to deny that Indians in British Columbia, as well as in other provinces, may have certain legitimate grievances.

The whole concept of Indian reservations in our country seems incompatible with a democratic society, in which each person should have equal rights, no more and no less than others. I do not suggest there is a quick and simple solution to the problems at this moment. What do I suggest is that in the District of Mackenzie of the Northwest Territories, apart from one small community within the town of Hay River, there are no Indian reservations, and that Indians and non-Indians should be taking part in the development of our Northland with equality of opportunity for all and special privileges for none.

Few people of European descent, I believe, have

better grounds for forming an opinion of the character and qualifications of Indians of the Mackenzie Valley than I have. I have lived with them for almost half a century and I have always been in a position of mutual social equality with them.

The ancestry of any human being, by itself, does not indicate a basic superiority or inferiority of an individual. I deeply resent the inference made by some people of European descent that Indian Canadians are somehow inferior to other humans. And it saddens me when Indians themselves believe they are inferior.

There is a mistaken belief among some Indians that any Northerner should be able to step from a life in the bush to the high paid professions and occupations of today. Most of us Northerners are presently not qualified to compete in these fields. We would be utterly confused in a nuclear physics laboratory or in designing an electronic computer. This fact has nothing whatever to do with our basic intelligence or our ability to learn.

Skills and knowledge are learned and *acquired*, they are not God-given to anyone of a particular skin colour. We all have to learn that only through effort and perserverance can we attain positions beside southern Canadians, whose only advantage is having been involved in the environment of western culture for a longer time than have we Northerners.

. Some northerners do not yet realize the relationship between effort and reward. I am weary of those who cry, "gimme-gimme-gimme." At a meeting and banquet of N.W.T. settlement council members, one member from Fort McPherson pestered me all evening with, "What have you done for us? What have you done for the Indians?"

My reply was, "I have my hands full in coping with my own problems, and it had never occurred to me, and still does not, that Indians, because they are Indians, require help any more than I do. Individuals, Indian or white, just need help and encouragement and education in different directions."

His attitude seemed to be, "You have everything, we have nothing, therefore you as some kind of superior person should spend your time in helping us unfortunate ones."

One of my objectives in this essay is to try to show that such an approach to the modern problems of 'natives' of the North makes any worthwhile solution completely unattainable. The attitude of inferiority makes it most difficult for members of the Indian community to take their rightful place with the rest of Northern Canadians in getting on with the job. In this regard, what gives hope to me for the future is the belief that the inferiority complex often expressed or implied by Indians is a tool which has to some degree been handed on to him by other Canadians. He is using it now in hopes of gaining advantages and bettering his position. My task is to convince the Indians that using this means of gaining their objectives is self-destructive.

Another hurdle to overcome is the idea that the good things of western society come without effort. Once a person has decided to accept the challenges of modern life on equal terms with other Canadians, he must come to realize his task has just begun. He is then merely on the starting line, as it were. There is a mind-boggling variety of good things in life which pass before our eyes almost daily. Part of the preparation for success in our society is in a realization that we must all limit our objectives in a realistic manner.

Any intelligent person knows that there are many items in the array of goods and services which we can never attain. Most of us will have to do without million dollar mansions, Lincoln Continentals, and regular trips to the Caribbean.

But, there are many things in the good life which are attainable. Those of us who have little hope of ever owning part of the means of production must adapt to an occupation, job or profession in order that we may legitimately share the wealth through salary or wages. Goods and services do not rain down on us in a shower from heaven. Minerals, water, soil and sunshine by themselves do not produce an apple pie or a skidoo. Man's brain, muscle and 'guts' make them available.

To fit ourselves for an occupation where we have a moral right to demand a share of the goods we see is not an easy task for anyone. It comes to mind that years ago, when I was a dog team trapper, a quantity of beautiful furs hanging in our cabin were being admired by a group of southern Canadians. They appeared to be slightly envious of the wealth displayed. They seemed to think all we did was to set a few traps around the door, then the lynx, marten and fox would line up to take their turn in stepping in the traps. Most northerners know that such is not the case. It was next to impossible to convey to those southerners the extent of toil and struggle of a trapper's life, the hardships and often suffering in extreme winter weather. In our daily work we were sometimes driven to the point of physical exhaustion. In those days we did not dwell on this aspect of the matter, but it was a dangerous life and took backbone and stamina to wrest a living from the bush in the days of the dog team.

The challenges of the present day are different in some ways, but compared to the life we previously led, they are 'a piece of cake'. It is true that the situation has changed, but the rules seem to be much as before. Instead of shovelling a ton of snow to clear a camp and cut down dry trees for firewood at the end of a long hard day when you are already exhausted, now you sit in a warm room, study diagrams and read books until the words blur and your head aches. Instead of having to cross a lake in a storm, you worry about the next academic exam or passing the welding test.

Indian leaders are saying that welfare and alcohol are destroying lives. It is undoubtedly true that the uncontrolled consumption of liquor is in fact ruining many people. It is not fair to couple welfare with booze in this respect. To my mind the beneficial effects of our system of welfare services far outweigh the ill effects from abuse of the services.

I think it is logical to assume that welfare and liquor are going to be with us in our society for the foreseeable future. We will have to learn to live with them.

Booze is available to all. Some will not use it at all. Some will drink a little and some drink a lot. You have a choice as to what extent you will indulge. We are people with will power, imagination and self-control. If any of us wish to indulge excessively we are at liberty to do so. If by doing so others are hurt, however, then a penalty has to be paid.

If a person will not respond to the rules and regulations laid down by the majority of the members of his community, then his freedom must be restricted. That is the reason for jails.

In cases where individuals will not restrict themselves in the use of alcohol, and persist in its abuse, then an interdicted list should be established. The right to purchase or consume liquor would be prohibited, regardless of personage. This rule should be rigidly, consistently and fully enforced. Living in the North among the people, together with my experience as a Justice of the Peace, has convinced me there is no other way to deal with the problem of alcohol abuse.

The Northwest Territories today is a good place to live for all residents, regardless of their ancestry. The money poured into this region over the last two decades for Medicare, education, vocational training and other projects has been staggering. Much of the financial help has gone to Indian groups and organizations. Financial figures and statistics can be boring, and we all know that statistics, charts and graphs can be confusing and can be manipulated to produce different conclusions. But often statistics are helpful to make a point. Allow me to quote from the *Northern Canada Business Directory* of 1976-77, "Financial Assistance Program Available from the Department of Economic Development & Tourism, Government of the Northwest Territories." Under the heading Indian Economic Development Fund. Purpose of the programme: "Loans and grants may be made available to help Canadian Indians in developing, maintaining and expanding viable business opportunities which in turn will provide job opportunities. Available to individuals, groups or bands, the programme provides loans up to $500,000, although this may be exceeded with the approval of the Treasury Board. There is no prescribed limit for grants, each case to be decided on its merits." Under the above statement is the name of J.A. Bergasse, Director.

Figures given by the department are listed by region, Inuvik, Fort Smith, Keewatin and Baffin. We are concerned only with the District of Mackenzie which includes Inuvik and Fort Smith. Loans listed under Small Business Loan Funds alone for the years 1970 to 1976 total $3,219,750.

Surely, there is no nation in the world doing more to expand the opportunities for a meaningful life and the pursuit of worthwhile objectives for its so-called 'native people' than Canada is doing in our North country.

Despite what southerners might hear to the contrary, increasing numbers of 'native people', men and women who vary in the colour of their skin from 'white' to light brown, are taking their place in the wage economy of an expanding North. Spokesmen for some groups are attempting to deny this fact.

They seem to advocate two or more separate ethnic cultures in northern Canada, with walls built around each. Some advocates of what could be termed 'northern separation' vehemently deplore the assimilation and integration which is taking place. The view is expressed that 'Indians' for some strange reason cannot or do not wish to take their place beside other Northerners in what one writer says is a "materialistic Canadian society, which is not long on human tendencies." With the pressure on Indians to retain their "identity" and their old way of life, whatever that means, it is not surprising that today there are some who say they are unable to compete in the wage economy.

Glenn Bell, speaking for the Brotherhood at the Berger Hearings, is reported to have said, "Wherever the special relationship that aboriginal people have with the land has been disrupted they have been affected by alcoholism, crime, family breakdown and poverty." And Cardinal says the white man has destroyed the Indian with welfare and alcohol. It seems that the new culture has introduced such a variety of temptations to the Indians that their lives have been ruined.

I submit that the crying over the misuse of the temptations of the world is in fact punitive rhetoric. If it were not, where would it lead us? When a man walks into a booze house and sits and drinks his paycheque away, and then curses down the 'white man' for putting the liquor outlet there, it would be like my blaming food stores for my over-eating.

So many people are killed by over-eating that perhaps we should indict the food stores on the charges of causing bodily harm. After all we would be able to show beyond a reasonable doubt that in the good old days before we were invaded by railroads, highways and chain stores, people did not die of over-eating. And by that line of reasoning the people who own the food stores must be found guilty of the charge. Lazy, incompetent students at university should perhaps blame those institutions of learning for having failed their examinations. They could argue that before the days of schooling they would not have suffered such indignities.

Would any judge listen with patience to a man who said, "Here I am on the stand, facing a charge of having killed a family on the highway when I was driving while impaired. Certainly I had consumed much alcohol. No one forced it down my throat. I drank of my own accord as I often do. But there is no way I am to be blamed for this habit of mine.

"In the good old days before my father was born there was very little alcohol available for people like me. Also there were no automobiles and no highways, and this sort of thing I am being charged with did not happen. The manufacturers of cars and the makers of alcohol should be standing here being tried for this crime, not me."

A neat argument, perhaps, but without much chance of standing up in court. If the lawyers of this man being charged were to continue with a lengthy dissertation on the theme of putting the blame for the crime on the purveyors of alcohol, then I would suspect that the court would politely ask them to desist.

The trick of blaming a group of people for the difficulties faced by another group has often been used. It has been a partially successful manoeuver especially when the group so accused is of a different colour, religion or political belief than the group making the accusations. It is well-known today how successful Adolf Hitler and other Fascists (some I believe in our own country) were in blaming the Jews for all the troubles of the world.

Some people blame the Communists for the woes of the world, or the country, or whatever; some blame the unions (any union will do); some blame the banks and other financial institutions; some blame the French; others blame those damned Englishmen.

Any excuse is good enough to put the blame for a particular problem somewhere else than where it belongs, and this is usually right where it is, on our doorstep. Another way of stating this is to suggest that the solution to many problems is with the ones who make the accusations.

But solutions are hard to come by. They often require searching self-analysis, intelligent thinking, forgiveness of the alleged enemy, devotion to your community and courageous action by a sufficient number of people to swing the tide.

It is much easier to look for a scapegoat, someone to censure and condemn, a target for the pent-up fury, the anger bubbles to the surface when human beings find themselves cornered by situations that are complex and frustrating.

Without the C.P.R. transcontinental railroad the development of the west would have been long delayed. It opened up large areas for farming and ranching. In spite of this, the C.P.R., possibly for good reasons, in some instances was held in low esteem by some farmers. One year the crops were very poor and one farmer had his total acreage devastated by drought, grasshoppers and gophers. A friend, in giving sympathy to him said, "Henry, it's a crying shame this had to happen."

And the farmer replied, "Yes it is. Damn the C.P.R."

I will attempt to show that in the North, the 'white man', who is blamed for all the problems of the Indians, is in the same category as the poor old C.P.R.. Some censure might be legitimate, but who can properly be blamed for the dry weather, or people drinking themselves to senselessness in a pub?

4

BERGER HEARINGS

In early 1974 with the 'land freeze' in effect in the District of Mackenzie, development was slowed down. The oil exploration industry was harassed by environmental nincompoops. Unemployment was increasing and many of us were wondering just what was going on. The Berger Commission was established against this background.

On March 21, 1974, the Privy Council of Canada appointed Mr. Justice Thomas Berger to—"inquire into and report upon the terms and conditions that should be imposed in respect to any right-of-way that might be granted across Crown lands for the purposes of the proposed Mackenzie Valley pipeline, having regard to the social, environmental and economic impact regionally of the construction, operation and subsequent abandonment of the proposed pipeline in the Yukon and Northwest Territories, and any proposals to meet the specific environmental and social concerns set out in the expanded Guidelines for Northern Pipelines as tabled in the House of Commons on June 28, 1972 by the Minister."

When Mr. Justice Berger was chosen to head the enquiry, and news of the appointment spread throughout the North, there was mixed reception. Clearly no one doubts the ability, integrity, and judicial qualifications of the man.

But how can his Enquiry be impartial when it seems that he is a quiet but determined exponent of so-called 'native rights' in Canada? Could it be that Mr. Berger would see here a chance to postpone the development of the District of Mackenzie and to ease the way for the Indian Brotherhood to pry vast sums of money from the workers and other taxpayers of Canada?

Many Northerners, on contemplating the appointment of Mr. Justice Berger, were apprehensive regarding the report he would bring out. What little he has said in public has not allayed those fears. He is reported to have said, "This Enquiry is not about a gas pipeline; it relates to the whole future of the North."

I do not pretend to have the formal education nor the legal training of Mr. Justice Berger. But I am one Northerner who is greatly concerned with the development of the area and all its people, and I can read and comprehend the English language.

To my understanding, Berger's responsibility is to enquire into the aspects of precisely the building of the pipeline. If his Enquiry relates to the whole future of the North, why not to the whole of Canada? Why do we need a Federal government if Mr. Berger thinks he has the responsibility for deciding the future of the North?

It is seldom indeed that we Northerners see or hear in the Canadian media an informed, impartial and objective opinion on Northern problems. I include the C.B.C. television and radio in this regard.

But in a recent issue of *Maclean's* Magazine, Barbara Amiel has won my heart with her clever and honest assessment of the whole issue of the Berger Enquiry. She says, in part, "A man of impeccable personal integrity and distinction on the bench, he nevertheless has built his career as an advocate of native land rights arguing landmark cases on the issue up to the Supreme Court of Canada. As one-time provincial leader of the British Columbia N.D.P. Party, he clearly came to the hearings with more than a casual affiliation to a party whose stand on control of resource development, multinational corporations (and evils thereof) was a matter of public record."

The fact that a person has or has not had an affiliation with any political party of Canada should have no bearing on the consideration of an appointment to a public enquiry. What I do suggest is that the past history of an appointee should show that he has an open mind on the questions to be examined. And I feel that in this case there is some doubt about it.

It was thought by many Northerners that the pipeline enquiry was to concern itself with the regional consequences of building the gas pipeline and the corridor, and only that. From following the newspaper, radio and TV reports given out it seems that the Enquiry has gotten completely out of hand.

The Berger Hearings started in the spring of 1974 and continued on into the fall of 1976. They were mainly of two kinds, formal and informal. The formal hearings in the North were held in Yellowknife, and at these hearings, parties were represented by lawyers and were open to cross-examination. Experts in many fields were called, questioned and examined. Among the experts were scientists, engineers, biologists, anthropologists and environmentalists.

Among the groups represented at the formal hearings were the consortium of companies with applications before the National Energy Board, the N.W.T. Indian Brotherhood and other 'native' organizations, the Legislature of the N.W.T., the Association of Municipalities of the N.W.T., the

Chamber of Commerce of the N.W.T.,and about fifteen other Northwest Territory groups and organizations.

The only solid and unqualified opposition to the pipeline was from the 'native' organizations, their advisers and people whom they brought forward.

In what I saw of the material presented by those with applications before the Energy Board, most of it was well researched and reasonable. Never before have I heard such a degree of concern expressed, with proof of that concern for people living in the area, by an industry involved with development of a region. Evidence was presented to indicate the seriousness of the application to build the pipeline. Canadian Arctic Gas has within the last four years spent $16,000,000 on environmental studies. They have spent an additional $30,000,000 on a test line in the Mackenzie Valley, with plans and technical studies. Arctic Gas claims, "The exploration-pipeline training programme in which we are active has already admitted 200 Northerners; another 120 are in at this moment (1977) and we have applications on file for yet another 400. More than eighty-five per cent of these are native people."

In summing up at the formal hearings, John Ballem, counsel for the consortium said, "Just as it is folly to proceed without sufficient information, so it is folly to delay until every last conceivable piece of information has been wrung dry."

Many others approved the building of the pipeline with reservations. Typical of the N.W.T. Government departments that gave reserved approval was the submission by the Director of Economic Development & Tourism for the N.W.T., who said in part, "If development of the North includes both economic growth and the proper extension of social and political institutions, then Northern development means "Opportunities for Northerners."

Heads of various Territorial Government departments gave evidence at the formal hearings of how their departments would be affected by the building of the pipeline, with details of how they were prepared to deal with developments which the pipeline would trigger.

There were more than 14,000,000 words recorded in the formal and informal hearings and I have only attempted to get information enough to present an outline of the arguments, both pro and con, regarding the contemplated construction of the pipeline.

The importance of the Mackenzie Valley Pipeline is perhaps second only in importance in the growth of Canada to the building of the transcontinental railroad by the C.P.R. One indication of this is the words of Mr. Justice Berger to a group in Calgary on September 20, 1975. He is reported to have said the pipeline route might constitute a corridor which might eventually include both a gas and an oil pipeline, a road, a railroad and a power transmission line.

When Mr. Berger spoke of the Mackenzie Pipeline Enquiry as embracing the whole future of the North, these were just the words certain pressure groups were waiting for. The Indian Brotherhood with the assistance of their southern advisers saw the opportunity to publicize what amounted to a tirade of alleged and imagined grievances against everything and everybody who did not agree with them.

This they did in the Berger Community Hearings which followed the formal ones. The Commission travelled to the various settlements in the District of Mackenzie to hear from anyone who wished to speak. The Community hearings were quite informal. From information that I have gathered I believe that the Indian Brotherhood sent representatives to the various settlements well ahead of the Hearings to marshal support and witnesses for their cause. I understand that some of the evidence was not as spontaneous as Mr. Berger was led to believe.

At the community hearings it seems that Mr. Berger was determined to hear without questioning a whole series of complaints directed against 'white' encroachment of 'native' lands. Here was the Big White Father listening in silence to his children. The Father who, with power from heaven, would lead his flock out of the wilderness. He would right the wrongs and end the oppression of his people by an encroaching industrial society.

Berger was patently unfair and unjust for two reasons. First, the publicity generated by the hearings in the news media is being focused on a facet of Northern conditions from one angle only, thus giving the impression to uninformed southerners that the District of Mackenzie is made up wholly of subjugated and unhappy aborigines. It has not been countered by sufficient information of a broader picture of the whole situation in the North. Therefore, I believe the Commission, and the Canadian public, have been led down the garden path. This will only serve the narrow purpose of the Indian Brotherhood. It will render legitimate information on construction of the pipeline, pro and con, more difficult to sort out, with the solution obscured by misplaced priorities.

Second, and of the utmost gravity, the Commission, by so obviously 'talking down' and 'acting down' to Northerners of Indian ancestry, perpetuates the false sense of insecurity or 'inferiority' that most Northerners deplore and have been trying to eradicate.

Indians and Metis are no fools. They can see as well as anyone the marked difference in the formal hearings, where a witness was cross-examined at every turn and could not get away with any unsubstantiated statements, and the informal hearings where it was obvious that those giving statements were looked upon as children or inferiors who were not expected to be able to defend their statements or opinions.

If I had been in their shoes I would have thought, "Here we go again. Because I am an Indian, and because I am not conversant in English, these people treat me as an aborigine. The condescension in their attitude and behaviour is hard to bear. Indeed, perhaps I am not equal to a 'white' man, so I will play their little game, and get what I can out of it."

The damage is done in inadvertently assuming a condescending attitude to certain Northerners because of economic status or ethnic origin, is unbelievably damaging to their ego. You have to live in the North among the people for years to be aware of this fact. But it is there and it is very real. And it is paramount that we lose no time in not only *saying* there is equality for every Northerner, but also *showing* that it is so by word and deed and *attitude*, especially by people from southern Canada, who are known to be respected by all Canadians.

I cannot help imagining a similar situation taking place in the old days in the hills of Kentucky and Arkansas, where a Commission is set up on the rocky hillsides, and moved from shack to shack, listening patiently to the aroused Hillbillys. After hearing volumes on the living conditions there, and complaints of the 'Revenooers' and the 'Feds', the Commission might reasonably conclude that these people, because of their ethnic Scottish and English ancestry, could not cope with the advancing western society, and were being subjected to prejudice and discrimination and should be handed vast sums of money to set up their own government, where they could live in peace and drink their corn whiskey without being harassed.

Different views were taken by Northerners in reference to 'living on the land' versus a 'wage economy'. For the native people of Coppermine, an Eskimo village east of the Delta where Gulf Oil

Canada operates a program employing native people in exploration activity, development and wage economy has helped secure the things which some claim that everyone wants, without disrupting so-called 'traditional' native ways. Four native people from Coppermine appeared before Mr. Justice Berger to urge that development not be deferred.

"If no development goes in the North, it will be very sad to many of us," said Lena Pederson, former member of the N.W.T. Legislative Assembly for the Coppermine area. "What is the future for our children? Do we expect that these children have to go somewhere else to look for jobs, or do we expect...that many small communities will close down because of no development?"

Red Pederson, chairman of the Coppermine Settlement council, said the employment program has been "generally most beneficial...I do not know of any complaints." He said that "the employment has not interfered with the traditional living off the land."

Bill Lafferty, a member of the N.W.T. Legislature and a Metis, told the Berger Hearings in Fort Simpson, "I personally see a great potential (for the North) in the pipeline."

The Metis Association of the N.W.T. split with the Brotherhood and made a submission of reserved approval of the building of the pipeline. Mr. Richard Hardy, president of the Association, said in part, "We cannot now endorse or suggest an economic future which will in any way hinder or adversely affect such an economic state. We therefore look to the construction of the pipeline as one of the major economic projects which we wish to take part in...If we as Metis people are to survive and to continue to grow socially and culturally, we must first be economically and otherwise secure." He went on to say that he did not see much of a future for the people in an exclusive life of hunting and trapping. Many Northerners consider the District of Mackenzie in the N.W.T. as their home. The spirit of adventure, the desire to take part in the expansion and development in a part of the country where a man could still be known by name and not by a number, was the motivation of others in coming up from the south. All who came have a willingness to work and become involved in the exciting future of the North. Some brought a small amount of capital to establish a business. Some, like myself, brought nothing and still have nothing of value except many friends and a deep love for the North and all its people.

I feel that most Northerners, whether born here or not, deeply deplore being pigeon-holed into separate racist compartments. Half the people of the North I know have some Indian blood or are married to a spouse who is part Indian. I notice an increasing tendency in Northerners to wish to be classed only as Canadians, and they do not wish to be marked with a brush of any colour. Most of us are fiercely nationalistic. We abhor any movement or propaganda that tends to split us into groups. We embrace all tendencies to eliminate whatever prejudice there has been in the past, and to weld us into a proud part of Canada.

In their opening statement to the formal Berger Hearings the Brotherhood stated, "Those assumptions are two: first, that gas from the Canadian Arctic will soon be needed in southern Canada; and second, that this pipeline is inevitable. We repeat, we do not accept these assumptions."

Later on, Raymond Yakaleya told the Berger Hearings in Norman Wells, "That gas and oil, that's ours...The land settlement of 450,000 square miles, that is our land, and realize it.....If the pipeline is built, at least half the production must remain in the economic control of the Dene people.

5

PIPELINE

The economic viability of the Mackenzie Valley pipeline is something the authorities of the National Energy Board will have to decide. Who will get the contract and what route seems best are matters outside the scope of this essay. Whatever their decision, there will always be some segment of the population that will be dissatisfied. I have no doubt the government will do whatever they think is best for Canada. It would seem futile to try to look too far ahead, and we should not expect them to make a decision based on what will be known fifty years from now.

What does concern us is the economic impact on the North, not only building the pipeline but, more importantly, what the existence of an energy and transportation corridor down the Mackenzie Valley will mean to the future of us all. Economic and social questions stemming from the existence of the corridor must concern every one of us. The future of the whole District of Mackenzie and the lives of thousands of Northerners yet unborn depends on our beginning the construction of the pipeline within the next two years.

Given the awareness of the importance of environmental studies by government, Arctic Gas and others, the environmental impact of the building of the corridor will be less damaging than what the general public is led to believe.

Because of the Berger Hearings and the publicity given to the Brotherhood propaganda by the news media, there is an awareness among Northerners that the pipeline could possibly be delayed long enough to cause hardship and suffering to the people of the District of Mackenzie. Therefore, it is incumbent upon those of us closest to the action to attempt to show that some of the arguments against building the pipeline are to a large extent false and misleading.

One likely outcome of the establishment of a Dene nation ruled by the Brotherhood strikes fury in my soul. Where would it leave the majority of the people who are now there? The so-called 'white' and Metis, most of whom are committed to a wage economy? No one has a desire to make 'little brown men' or 'little white men' out of Indians or anyone else for that matter. We should all be classed as Northerners with no walls, buckskin or propaganda curtains built to separate us. The Brotherhood implies that the Dene nation would be for Indians only and that the rest of us could get out.

A speech given by R.D.S. Ward suggest the future establishment of provincial status for the N.W.T., through the democratic process of one man, one vote. Personally I would go one step farther and suggest provincial status for the District of Mackenzie, where in time we will not think of one another as men and women of different races, but as people, Northerners, Canadians.

It was sad to read Mr. Justice Berger's address to the Southern Alberta Institute of Technology, where he twice referred to the pipeline which would cross the land where four different races live. Surely today, in all the world, in all Canada, and in our Northland, we are trying to get away from that racist business. With the help of the majority of Northerners, our administration in Yellowknife is making great strides in this direction.

Here is an examination by an expert on the possibilities stemming from mineral resources of the District of Mackenzie, provided a transportation corridor is opened down the Mackenzie River to the Arctic. The following is a personal quote from Mr. C.C. Lord, Nahanni District Geologist, Northern Affairs, Yellowknife:

"These are the impressions of what might happen, given—

a A different government and private industry attitudes.

b The need to truly develop the North is seen by Ottawa, and not just token gestures.

c The native people are made fully aware of what the results will be and what benefits there are to all. i.e. don't stall.

d The commodities I mention below are not economic at present level but they might be one day if the demand and foresight is given to each project.

1 Mining—There are several major deposits of lead-zinc in carbonate rocks in the Mackenzie Mountains which if given the same logistics as down south, would now be mines.

2 Problems—We are in need of the following to develop the Mackenzie Valley and mountain area—

(a) Transportation—roads, railways, etc.

(b) Power (HEP). Power is needed to process the ore because operations in the North have generally to be twice as rich and large as in the south. More tons per day have to be mined to make a profit. Therefore, large amounts of power must be available.

(c) There must be a reliable work force available.

3 There are several rivers which could possibly be

used for hydro electric power, i.e. Little Bear River.

4 There is a large deposit of iron ore at the Snake River area. Although the world has plenty of iron ore, what is needed is steel. Possibly with the combination of iron ore at the Snake River, coal at Fort Norman with water and power of the Little Bear River, a steel plant might be built which would have a ready market for the end product.

5 Energy—There is a very favourable area for uranium exploration along the Mackenzie Valley, but unfortunately there is not much rock outcrop and hence exploration would be very expensive. However, if we need the U-308 bad enough we can find it.

6 Coal—There are sizable deposits of reasonable thermal 'rank' coal around the Fort Norman and Little Bear areas, which could possibly be used for degasification as in northern Ontario, or possible fuel source for domestic use.

7 Let us forget the myth that because things are in the North, it is expensive to get them out. There is a natural expense because of transportation, but it appears to be an expense of, say 15 to 20 per cent just because it is in the North. We should try to change attitudes and make people realize Northwest Territories is approximately one third of Canada in area. And unless development begins soon it may be too late to suddenly 'attack' the North and sensibly exploit its riches. There are enough commodities up here to spread around.

These impressions are perhaps part of a dream I have for the North and its development and possibly a long way down the line. But—damn it—if the Russians can do it and apparently make it work, why can't we?"

Chris Lord—Yellowknife—Feb. 1977

Mr. Lord has shared with us his dream. It is a dream that many Northerners have. Do not scoff at his dream, for any worthwhile endeavour which man has ever attempted has started out with a dream.

The dream that many Northerners have today of a bright and dramatic future where we and our children can emerge from an existence of drudgery and privation into a land of equal opportunity, with fair and just rewards for all, is at last coming true. Sit for a while in the Council Chambers of the Northwest Territories Legislature and listen to the discussion and debates. See the variety of people, the many opinions and points of view expressed in an atmosphere of, "We are one big family. We have problems. We will thrash them out and then get on with it." Visit the government offices where exciting new programs, with generous funding, are getting young people started in building the North. Visit the Mackenzie Highway construction camps (until they were shut down) and see the men and women from far reaches of the North working together in a spirit that gives the lie to those who cry, 'white', 'Indian', 'bigotry', 'prejudice' and 'discrimination'. Visit the regional government offices where beautiful girls of local background make your eyes pop. See who is driving the bulldozers and earth-moving machines: men from the Arctic, the Mackenzie delta, Fort Norman and Fort Simpson. Dare not try to stop us. We are building the "True North, Strong and Free."

6

DISRUPTIVE FORCES

It is more in sorrow than anger that I now must deal with what I term disruptive forces that are directing the North into retrogression instead of progress. Racist propaganda is likely the most damaging of all. We have sufficient difficulties already in building and improving our Northern society without being hobbled with divisive forces. I see it as a battle between divisive and constructive forces.

Bill Lyle of the N.W.T. Legislative Assembly is a constructive force. He said at a N.W.T. council session in January of 1977, "I am an Eskimo, and I do not want any special status or privileges." He went on to say, and I quote from memory, "The people of Fort McPherson are screaming for more government funds for housing and more money for their airport. How is it that they are reported to be in opposition to building of the Mackenzie Valley pipeline, and at the same time feel justified in asking for government fund for their community? I cannot see that their views are consistent. I cannot see the reason for their opposition to the pipeline."

Some day soon men like Billy Lyle will be the leaders in a new province of Mackenzie, and I think that if the truth were known the people he speaks of are not against the building of the pipeline.

There are many people in the North today who are embarrassed by the Brotherhood propaganda that encourages all with Eskimo or Indian blood to reject western society, to wear buckskin coats and headbands and try to retain a separate identity. There seems to be nothing harmful to our society in the wearing of headbands, or leggings, or feathers or whatever. Our East Indians wear turbans, and Ukranian Canadians wear their beautiful dance costume. These customs add richness and colour to our society. But when the Brotherhood wishes to set up a Dene nation within Canada, we should fight the suggestion with every legal means at our disposal.

The spokesmen who unfailingly refer to the Canadian Government and all Canadians except themselves as 'white men' are being deliberately racist in this regard. At other times and in other parts of the world 'black' men have borne the brunt of frustrations of those of different colour. With some subtlety and cunning the phrase 'white man' is being used as a club to bring discredit to the North and sympathy to people of a different colour.

The days are long gone when the colour of a person's skin can be used as an argument against him. The southern advisers to the Brotherhood are fully aware of this and their use of implied racism is, to my mind, reprehensible.

The spokesmen for the Brotherhood have three key objectives: Firstly, an unqualified opposition to the building of the Mackenzie pipeline is consistently expressed. The Berger Hearings should be for the purpose of hearing all suggestions and criticisms regarding the project, whether they are reasonable or ridiculous. Part of the work of the Enquiry should be to sort out the wheat from the chaff. When an argument seems to hinge on misleading information and belligerent opposition only, it should be labeled for what it is.

The Brotherhood spokesmen seem to be very concerned with convincing the Berger Commission, the press, the media and the southern Canadian public that their views are the *only* views on the subject held by the Indians of the Mackenzie Valley. No one knows to what degree the views expressed by the Brotherhood are supported by the ordinary Indian citizen. Many are coerced in one way or another into withholding their opinions. One object of this essay is to give heart and support to those who have not been heard. The Brotherhood have the money (from the Federal Treasury), the almost unanimous support of the news media, and have the backing of some well known southern Canadians. They therefore have the clout necessary to subdue and stifle views other than their own.

Some of the objections and complaints expressed by Indian spokesmen to the Berger Commission have been reported in the *Vancouver Sun* of November 19, 1976, in an article headed "Settle claims first, Indians tell Berger." Quotations follow:

"Indians of the Northwest Territories and the Yukon declared Thursday there should be no natural gas pipeline up the Mackenzie Valey until native claims are settled."

Do you notice that the report says 'Indians of the Northwest Territories'? Then it goes on to say that Glenn Bell was doing the talking. No doubt he was speaking for *some* Indians. But *all* of them, as implied? It seems doubtful. Would the *Vancouver Sun* report a speech by Joe Clark to the Progressive Conservative National Convention under the heading "White men demand resignation of Prime Minister Trudeau'?

To continue with the *Sun* report, "The Indian Brotherhood of the Northwest Territories branded the proposals cultural genocide and said they could not even discuss them until they'd had a chance to discuss their own fate.

"And the council of Yukon Indians said the significance of the native claims is that the claims will block construction and leave the people to their own lives.

"Glenn Bell speaking for the Brotherhood said the Dene people of the Northwest Territories have long been aware of the steady erosion of their lives by a variety of projects which have erroneously been described as development.

"Although these projects have had a destructive impact on the Dene, none by themselves threatened the very survival of the Dene in a way that the proposed Mackenzie Valley pipeline so clearly does."

In this vein the lamentations go on and on.

The article continues, "The cost should be measured in terms of the existence of a people, a nation, and in terms of the sanctity of human rights, none of which can be assessed through the mere application of capitalistic logic."

Really, Mr. Bell! Either your thinking is muddled, or you are trying to confuse your audience. Whatever the merit or demerit of the capitalistic system may be, they have nothing whatever to do with Indian land claims, the building of the pipeline or the wild talk of a separate Dene nation within the borders of Canada. In the world today there is a growing concern for human dignity and the rights of all for economic and political freedom. You would be hard put to argue conclusively that any political system by itself is more conducive to progress in this matter than another.

In Canada under any political system that would be voted into power the sanctity of human rights and dignity will continue to grow and expand. If we have not yet evolved to an ultimate degree of human liberty in our society, you cannot lay the blame on capitalism. For within the framework of our system we have made notable advances.

We have freedom of thought and of speech. Note the way in which the Brotherhood spouts off. Freedom from what? Look at our welfare system and Medicare, and old age pensions. Our educational system enables *any* Canadian to attain proficiency in his chosen field if he has the mental equipment and the resolve to work.

More quotes from the *Sun* are: "What the Dene are seeking," Bell said, "is their recognition of the right of self-determination within Confederation and the establishment of the necessary institutions, legal protection and official practices which will give full effect to that right.

"The Dene have suffered from white arrogance since 1798 when they showed the explorer Alexander Mackenzie the way down the great river to the Arctic Ocean," Bell said.

"He said the Dene people seek to retain the right to retain ownership of as much of their traditional land as required to insure their independence and self-reliance.

"He said that when the special relationship that aboriginal people have with the land has been disrupted, they have been affected by alcoholism, crime, family breakdown and poverty.

"Many Indian people feel they have no alternative now but to react violently to threats of development, Ron Veale told Mr. Justice Thomas Berger. Veale, speaking for the Council of Yukon Indians, said the very life of the Indians of the Old Crow community in the Yukon is threatened by pipeline plans."

What the Yukon Indians want, according to Mr. Veale, is to block construction of the pipeline and leave the people to their own lives. Development, he says, has meant a steady erosion of their lives. And Mr. Bell says the Indians have been affected by alcoholism, family breakdown and poverty.

Has development really brought alcoholism,

family breakdown and poverty? Surely a truer assessment would be that some people allowed themselves to slip into a world of drugged escape when they found themselves dissatisfied and frustrated with their new environment. Crime and family breakdown seem to follow the excessive use of alcohol and/or drugs. When a man's money goes to the liquor store and the booze house, naturally he has less for food and clothing. Most of those who complain of poverty today would have died an early death from sheer incompetence in the Stone Age.

Many people beside Indians in our country are having difficulties in adjusting to our changing society. They are not alone. Each of us is faced with some difficulties in acceptance of the changing pace.

The problem has nothing to do with an individual's ancestry. Some adjust to a changing environment more easily than others. Vast numbers of young people in our cities have been seduced into the world of drugs and have committed suicide. Older people have taken the same way out when faced with money and family problems. There are increasing numbers of mental patients within institutions and borderline cases on the streets.

Let us not delude ourselves. We are all paying one fearful price for the material and technological advances of the day. Clearly there is as much pressure on those of us at the bottom of the ladder as there is on those at the top.

And it is also self-evident that we are stuck with our way of life and all its problems. Nobody wants to do without electricity, swift transportation, Medicare, indoor plumbing and shopping centres with their abundance of items. And the proof that Northerners, 'natives' if you will, are as hooked on our modern way of life as everyone else is that the people of the North crowd into settlements where the amenities in every direction around the settlements. But no one is living there.

If jobs and opportunities for young people can be provided, the future of Northern towns looks bright. We need the work and activity which development will provide, and which it will if we get busy and plan for it now.

Mr. Bell says he needs much land to give him independence and self-reliance. You cannot expect to have independence and self-reliance, Mr. Bell, handed to you. Each is a quality which an individual builds and strengthens within himself through his own efforts. Oil revenues, blackmailed from other Canadians, will not build self-reliance.

Perhaps the money and land which the Brotherhood is manoeuvering for from the public treasury will have the opposite effect to the supposed beneficiaries. Pride, self-reliance and independence might be destroyed.

Independent and self-reliant men are often with limited worldly goods. They are independent because they are self-reliant. In the North, one of the most self-reliant and independent men I know is an Indian who was born at Fort Chipewyan. He was very poor. I worked beside him for thirty years. Today he is successful and respected throughout the North.

One of the major disruptive forces to our Northern society if the view, expressed and implied, that there is one group of Canadian who because of their Asian ancestry, cannot fit themselves into our advancing society. Others say it is because they have recently emerged from the Stone Age and find themselves left behind in the race for status, material goods and position. They point to the fact that many Canadians of Indian ancestry are on the lower rung of the economic ladder. Their families are breaking up and many have taken to alcohol. Some have a hard time holding jobs and some are on welfare.

From the foregoing, two damaging assumptions are made. First, it is forgotten that the majority are showing that they *can* and *are* adjusting to a changing environment. The assumption that seems to be implied in some views is that Indians are inferior to other Canadian and cannot hope to compete. It should be evident that this is a dangerous and mistaken concept, and the sooner we let it go, the sooner we find a solution to the problems of the North.

The principal requirement in laying the foundation for a healthy Northern society is the clearing away of the now-antiquated attitude that anyone by virtue of ancestry is either suited or unsuited for any particular occupation.

Canadian Indians are no better at hunting or skinning an animal than a French Canadian or an Italian Canadian. Conversely, Indian Canadians can and will over the next two decades show that they can take their place beside others in the higher professions of our society. Some already are lawyers, doctors, engineers and artists.

Secondly, it is alleged that racism, prejudice and discrimination hold Indians back from attaining status in the community. If it were ever true, it is no longer so in the North today.

One man in giving his views to the Berger Enquiry said that for many years he had stood on the banks of the Mackenzie River and had seen many barge loads of freight move down the river and past his village, loaded with thousands of tons of equipment and consumer goods. Not once did the barges stop to unload even a small portion of goods for him. And furthermore whenever this man was in Fort Simpson, where on rare occasions the barges did stop to unload, there was never anything for him or his people.

From this he assumed he was living in an unfair 'white man's' society, and something was very wrong. Surely he was being extremely naive. He knew that the freight from the barges is delivered to retail outlets or to government departments. And it did not occur to him to mention that he lives in a tiny settlement forty-five miles from the nearest village and that the fifty-six people who live there have a heavily subsidized diesel electric plant providing power to each household, a day school with a resident teacher plus medical and police services either visiting or flown in when needed. At the settlement is a sawmill, heavily subsidized by the Territorial Government, which provides work for the men of the community.

"It seems to me that the best way to control our resources is through Provincial status; in other words, within the framework of the presently attainable democratic process. If this is not immediately attainable, then a time frame within which it will be attainable should be developed and people should prepare for that development.

"Meanwhile it is incumbent on the Government of Canada to (a) treat all residents as citizens of Canada with the same rights and responsibilities, and (b) set aside a portion of the Royalties from the exploitation of our natural resources in the form of a trust fund, to be turned over to us when Provincial status is obtained. That way, the new Northern Province could at least begin on a sound economic base. "The native peoples, being in the majority, would have the dominant say in our new Province, through the duly elected representatives to that provincial government, and within our present democratic process. Any other way could lead to anarchy and chaos. We need only look at the province of Quebec where it can be said that the majority rules, as with the French-speaking Quebecers.

"When Newfoundland became a province, native Newfoundlanders dominated the provincial government, and do so to this day. We are lucky to live in this country, but we must remember that together with the benefits of our society goes the terrible

77

responsibility of donating to that society, not merely taking from it. Those who continually seek ways of taking from society will eventually destroy that society. It seems today that more and more people are speaking of division and special status. Stronger language is being used and this can only cause hardship and social unrest. Surely, responsible citizens should look for means to compromise without the use of inflammatory rhetoric.

It has been written, 'However you shall show, so shall you reap'. It is incumbent on the Government of Canada and the leaders of the Indian communities to sit down together and come to terms in settling the problems facing us. The British Common Law recognizes 'Squatters Rights' and that, together with the broad outlines of the Treaties and the generosity of the people of Canada, should resolve the problem. In summing up, Land Claims, yes, within limits, and as soon as possible. Native sovereignity, no. There is no place in the democratic nation for another government outside our present system, unless it is a government for all the people in the North, and by that, I mean, provincial status."

If the Indian Brotherhood were doing their job, they would have informed the complainant that all Northern communities, including his own, were extremely fortunate to have the modern facilities which they have, and that the people of the settlement do actually receive more than their fair share of the goods that move down the Mackenzie.

It will be interesting to hear what Mr. Justice Berger said or thought of the above presentation which was made to him verbally. If this man's implied wish to partake of the wealth of the country without contributing anything is indicative of the attitude of the Brotherhood, then it is high time that someone informed them that their position is clearly unsound.

Perhaps the federal government itself has contributed to the false concept that some people, because they have been resident in the country all their lives, have some God-given right to sit idly by, while others earn a living for them. Perhaps too much for too long has been handed them on a platter and they have become convinced it is their rightful due.

7

PEOPLE PROBLEMS

The allegation that prejudice and discrimination toward Indians are to be blamed for the social conditions of some Indian people of the North today warrants some discussion. How valid is the allegation that 'white' arrogance has held back the Indian?

Most human beings at one time or another manifest some degree of prejudice. Prejudice toward someone or something is likely present in all of us. It will be most minimal where opinions and feelings are based on 'reason'. To what extent does it exist in the Mackenzie Valley today?

At one time Indians throughout the North were classed as 'minors' and were wards of the government. As a consequence they did not have the right to vote or to consume alcohol. "Prejudice" screamed some. "Reasonable" said others, as they deemed Indians to be somewhat childish and naive. It was thought they could not handle alcohol and must be protected. Right or wrong, the policy soon came to an end and today all Northerners have equal legal rights with other Canadians. It should have been a step in the right direction. But what happened?

With legal access to liquor, drinking became

rampant among Indians, and to some extent non-Indians. If you doubt the inference that the problem is greater among Indians, go into any Northern town where the population is equally Indian and non-Indian. Keep your mouth closed and your eyes and ears open for a week or two and you will see the truth.

In one Northern village alone, with a population of under 1,200, since the opening of the liquor outlets there, there are reported to have been twenty deaths among Indian people which are directly or indirectly related to the misuse of alcohol.

Here are some recent statistics on consumption of alcohol at different centres within the Northwest Territories, in the fiscal year ending March 31, 1976. Population figures are from the latest official estimates. Liquor sales are from the Annual Report of the N.W.T. Liquor Control System, and the Liquor Licensing Board. Figures are approximate.

Total Annual Liquor Sales (1976) . . . . . $10,795,819.
Total Population—N.W.T.
    April 1977 estimates. 46,500

Liquor Outlet	Othere Settlements Served	
Yellowknife—	Rae-Edzo (voted dry 1976)...	$380 per capita
Norman Wells—	Fort Norman—Fort Franklin... (possibly Ft. Good Hope)	$233 per capita
Fort Simpson—	Ft. Liard—Nahanni Butte—... Jean Marie River—Wrigley	$350 per capita
Pine Point—	Ft. Resolution...	$250 per capita
Hay River—	Providence—Enterprise...	$300 per capita
Inuvik—	Aklavik—Tuktoyaktuk...	$385 per capita

Taking the above figures, say, for Fort Simpson, the amount spent on alcoholic beverages in a year for a family of five would be $1,750. If you subtract the families who do not drink (there are some) and those who drink moderately, and the three children from a family of five, the alcohol consumed by many adults is immense.

Comparative figures for the provinces are as follows and are taken from the 1973 statistics.

British Columbia..........................$110 per capita
Saskatchewan...........................$103 per capita
Alberta.....................................$115 per capita
Ontario.....................................$107 per capita
Northwest Territories....................$200 per capita

Since 1973, liquor sales in the Northwest Territories has increased by forty-one per cent, and the price increase has been approximately thirty-three per cent. (This does not include price increases for 1977.)

Again, looking over the statistics for the settlements in the Northwest Territories, it seems obvious that if those who complain of poverty were to spend their money on food instead of booze, there would in fact be little poverty in the Northern settlements.

In the last few years the government has been making a sustained effort to prepare Northerners for lower and middle management positions. Up to the end of 1976 there had been fifty people so trained. By April of 1977 the number of trainees will be increased by another fifty, giving a total of 100.

Keep in mind that the total population of the Northwest Territories is about 45,000, equal to the population of one good sized town in southern Canada.

Officials of the department say that so far there has been from sixty to seventy per cent success in the training of native people for management positions, with the percentage of success going up each year. This one fact alone gives the lie to those who say that 'natives' are offered only jobs in the unskilled occupations in the development programs of the North.

How can anyone expect to walk out of the bush into a top government job? It takes years of training and service to attain management positions either within a government service or with a private company.

There are many Federal and Territorial Government departments in the N.W.T. with headquarters at Yellowknife and with branches throughout the Territories in most towns and settlements. These departments deal with manpower, health and welfare, community development and administration. Many positions of field and office personnel in these departments as well as local government are filled by Indians who are doing a good job. Many Indians are also employed on a salaried basis with Northwest Lands and Forests, Department of Public Works both Federal and Territorial, and the Crown Corporations of Canadian National Telecommunications and the Northern Canada Power Commission. All have gigantic payrolls within the District of Mackenzie, and each year sees an increase in the number of Northerners employed.

A theme that keeps re-occurring in the writings of some Indian leaders is that all the trouble that Indian people face today can be laid at the door of "white man's culture" and "white" arrogance. It is assumed that if Europeans had never invaded North America, Indians would still be living in their fondly imagined Utopia. The solution which some leaders present seems extremely unrealistic.

They advocate a 'nation' of their own, but within Confederation, and with funds handed them by the Federal government. Funds for what? They got along fine, they say, without the 'white man's' money for hundreds of years, and if the conditions of life was then so good, why mess it up now with funds? Would not money bring on the very same problems from which they allegedly wish to escape today? Administration, they say, will make the difference. They will escape 'white' arrogance and all will be rosy again.

A few points are forgotten. If Indians have not the qualifications today to be administrators in government, how do they expect to be qualified overnight?

And do they imagine that they can do without the expertise in the fields of medicine, mechanics, electronics, transportation and road construction and many others? It is childish to assume that they can set themselves apart and retain all the benefits and products of western culture without having to face the problems which that culture brings.

And how do they justify the demand for vast sums of money to keep their new nation flourishing? Simple. There is a vast wealth of oil, gas and minerals in the North which they claim by right of being here before Christ. It could be pointed out that if other Canadians had not come and brought the despised 'white' culture, Canadian Indians would still be roaming in nomadic tribes over the fields of undiscovered gas and oil, coal and minerals (which were useless to them) starving, suffering and barely able to exist with their rawhide snares and stone axes: running in fear from other tribes, and warring with them occasionally; with lives ruled by super-stition; women treated with cruelty and degradation; where soap was unknown and the use of water for cleansing was shunned.

The point cannot be escaped that all our ancestors, no matter of what origins, lived that way at sometime in the past. It is no credit or shame to anyone of us now. But it is also a blessing that we emerged from that primitive condition into what is now termed our modern culture.

Never once have I heard expressed in the writings of an Indian Brotherhood leader an appreciation of any of the multitude of goods, inventions and improvements in life brought by the 'white' man, and which enabled the people for whom he purports to speak to emerge from a Stone Age existence. And until I do hear such an admission, I am not able to take their vitriolic criticism of present-day society, or their tearful lamentations with much more seriousness.

Spokesmen refer repeatedly to the problems faced by Indians today, and imply it is 'white' prejudice or arrogance that is holding them back. No doubt they find themselves faced in daily life with puzzling and difficult decisions, and feel a longing for the past. They are not alone. Many others, in and out of the North, when faced by pressures of life, also look back on the by-gone days with nostalgia. Certainly there seems to be some good features in the pre-industrial way of life which we are in danger of losing. But in assessing the values of cultures, old and new, we should be realistic and practical. There is no gain to be made in deluding ourselves into thinking we can return to the past. The future will be good if we make it so.

References made to 'white arrogance' and 'white man' imply that our western culture is a culture of fair skinned people only. How wrong that is. The electronic age, technical society, space age or whatever, is enveloping the whole world. It is not 'white', 'black', or 'green'. The Arabs are now rich and pressuring us. The Africans are becoming increasingly involved in our so-called 'western culture'. The Yellow race has contributed much to the advancing world. Many Canadians are not exactly 'white'. For Goodness sake, if it is only the 'whites' you hate, say so; and if it is the technical age of automobiles, television, disease control, advancing knowledge and the plethora of material goods that you despise, then be precise.

Does anyone really believe that Indians, generally speaking, cannot cope with our culture? It is sometimes implied that everyone else simply breezes along in the world today without encountering serious difficulties, and that only Indians have problems. Nothing could be farther from the truth. Among the 'whitest' people in the world there is a staggering number who could claim that they cannot cope with the pressures of the modern world. Ulcers and frustrations drive many to an early grave. Institutions are overflowing with people who cannot cope with present conditions. The number of family break-downs is sky-rocketing. The incidence of known alcoholics is increasing all over the world. Many 'white' people want desperately to get out of the city, into the bush, back to nature to escape the rapidly changing world.

Canadian Indians of the Mackenzie basin, are you really saying that you cannot accept the challenge of modern life, and cannot do as well as the rest of us? Do you really believe the old hog-wash that Indians are inferior? Inferior to what, or to whom? What is inferior? Each of us is either inferior or superior in some way to someone else. What difference does that make? There will always be people who are better at some jobs than others. Most of us can never hope to be celebrities or to be rich and famous.

Indians do not have to take a back seat because their eyes are brown. There is an increasing number of Canadian Indians who have proven they are as good as the next man.

You hear the world 'Dene' mentioned quite often. It is the word the Mackenzie Indians used to describe themselves. It means 'Real Men'. They knew it then that they are real men and they know it now. We must rid ourselves of that which I call the Indian teepee syndrome, which is the erroneous concept that Indians are characterized by their inherent ability to paddle canoes, skin beaver, or tan a hide.

The truth is that a banker's child from London, England, when born will have no more or less of the inherent ability to paddle a canoe than a child born of Eskimo parents a Tuktoyaktuk. Under the same environment and training there is no way to tell which one, when mature, will be the better electronic engineer, or paddler.

8

HUNTING
AND
TRAPPING RIGHTS

One issue repeated over and over in the Berger Hearings was the demand by Indian leaders for the continuation of hunting, trapping and fishing rights in the North. Although the revenue from fur trapping is becoming economically less important as the North become industrialized, there are still many Northerners who depend on wild meat to supplement their diet. Many attempt to get at least one animal a year for their larder.

The quantity of wild game obviously is limited. As our population expands, the hunting pressure mounts, making it imperative that hunting 'rights' for all Northerners be reviewed.

The question of hunting and trapping rights today is far different from what it was in the Stone Age, or even at the time the Treaties were signed. The Stone Age natives were relatively few in number. They did not have the capability of hurting the caribou herds in those days. Unlimited hunting rights today are unrealistic. It would be a serious mistake to suggest, with the increasing population of Northerners and improved access to game, that unrestricted hunting rights should continue to exist.

Wildlife reserves simply cannot stand large numbers of people hunting game with modern methods the whole year through. The caribou herds in Alaska are a case in point.

From information from the Alaska Department of Fish and Game, we have these astounding facts. The Western Arctic caribou herd, estimated at between 240,000 and 260,000 in 1070, had declined in 1975 to 100,000 animals. By 1976, in one year's time, the herd, after extensive research, was estimated to be only 50,000 animals, including calves.

A complete closure on all killing of caribou was undertaken by the authorities, effective August 14, 1976.

Here are some related quotes from the Alaska Government news release of July, August and September, 1976.

"Proposals for the new regulations will include season restrictions, a bag limit of one bull, restricting the area open to hunting, and regulations for harvest by a permit system. Also to be considered are proposals banning the barter of caribou and their use for dog food. Additional restrictions on season and bag limits will also be proposed for the Porcupine caribou herd in the eastern Arctic.

"Rausch (Robert A. Rausch, Game Division Director) said that the department did not know all the factors causing the decline of the caribou, but that it was obvious that the take by both hunters and wolves was excessive at this time and would have to be curtailed.

"In other action the Board directed the Department to implement a control programme for wolves which have been taking an estimated 10,000 to 15,000 caribou from the Western Arctic herd. Village representatives as well and Department biologists testified that wolf populations have increased substantially in some areas, and wolves alone are now taking more than the annual increase in caribou in the Western Arctic.

"Extensive research in the spring and summer of 1976 resulted in population estimates of 52,000 caribou including calves. The combined take by humans and wolves during the 1975-76 season may have exceeded 40,000 animals. Based on this and other written and oral testimony, the Alaska Board of Game concluded that every possible means of reversing the decline should be taken. The decline if allowed to continue could possibly end with the complete decimation of the herd."

This information would seem to indicate that so-called 'natives' are no more responsible in game conservation than are people from the city. In some settlements in the North the people depend to some extent for their meat supply on caribou, moose and other wildlife, and should, one would think, be concerned with maintaining that supply.

Improved access, especially to caribou herds, will necessitate the immediate revision of our game regulations in the Canadian Arctic before we are faced with the situation that they now have in Alaska.

Appropriate legislation, with rigid control, is the answer to the dangers wildlife faces in those areas which are vulnerable to over-hunting.

If those Northerners termed 'native', Eskimo or 'Indian' are allowed to continue with their so far unrestricted right to hunt big game throughout the year, there will soon be no game to hunt. Therefore, whatever legislation the N.W.T. Legislative Assembly sees fit to enact must apply equally to all Northerners. Unrestricted slaughter of game *must* soon give way to a controlled program precisely for the reason of maintaining a supply of game for those who really need it.

Leaving the Barren Land caribou problem, let us

now go to the boreal forest area of the Mackenzie Valley, which comprises most of the Liard River and Mackenzie River area. Here the Indians have hunting, trapping and fishing rights that can hardly be extended any farther. Here the government's encouraging trappers in every possible way to get out into the bush. There are Trapper's Loans, or Trappers' incentive grants (fur subsidy), organized caribou hunts, and Hunters' and Trappers' Association administrative grants.

1 "Trappers' Loans—Our 'Trappers Assistance Program' is an ongoing loan program that provides non-interest loans to trappers for the purpose of outfitting themselves for the trapping season. It is normally used for food supplies, trapping equipment and transportation. Loans are to be repaid the following year. Total funds budgeted annually is $60,000. Mackenzie Valley residents are the prime users of the program in amounts up to $50,000 annually.

*Footnote—Many trappers nowadays like to fly to and from their traplines from a settlement by aircraft. Most do not want to spend any more time away from a settlement than is necessary.

2 "Trappers' Education Programmes—is an ongoing programme that was generally run by our field officers. The funds for the Mackenzie Valley amounted to $5,900 for the last fiscal year. We now have a Conservation Education Officer on staff and we expect a rapid acceleration of this program plus adequate funds to include the whole trapping community as well as interested groups of school children.

3 "Organized Caribou Hunts—Mackenzie budget $27,000. This program is to assist native communities in attaining caribou which would otherwise be inaccessible. The funds are mainly used to transport groups of community hunters into the caribou migration areas, and for the transporta-

tion* of meat back to the settlements. The hunts are generally organized by Fish and Wildlife officers to insure the most efficient use of the allocated moneys.

Footnote—Again the transportation is by air, covering many hundreds of miles.

4 "Trappers' Incentive Grants—(Fur Subsidy). This is an ongoing approved programme of fur subsidy to Northwest Territory trappers and is meant to be an incentive to greater production and to reduce the requirement for loans. The qualifying fur income range is between $400 and $2,000 with the subsidy being a variable percentage (approximately ten to twenty-five per cent) based on how the available funds relate to production and fur prices. Annual fur production varies between one million and three million dollars. The number of N.W.T. Trappers usually qualifying for a subsidy is approximately 1,500.

N.B.—Average production for the last nineteeen years is $1,400,000. Incentive funds paid in the Mackenzie Valley is $131,633.43.

5 "Hunters' and Trappers' Association Administration Grants—This is an ongoing annual grant to provide a small amount of administrative support to active Hunters' and Trappers' Associations. It is supplemented by funds they raise themselves. Delegates to regional H.T.A. conferences are financed with this funding. There are 17 H.T.A.s within the Mackenzie Valley. The grant was $500 for each H.T.A. The present requirements dictate that we should increase the grants to at least $1,500 per association."

One may gather from the above that the vast wilderness of the Mackenzie Valley is not exactly crawling with trappers.

The failure of the Government to persuade Indians to engage in hunting and trapping activities is related to the fact the Indians, young and old, male and female, do not want to return to such an existence. Young Indians of today are no more fitted for a life in the bush than are other young people of the 1970s. Most of them realize that their future does not lie in that direction. It is a mistake to assume that because many Indians have trapped and hunted in the past that they are necessarily fitted for such an occupation now. Would you tell all those beautiful Indian girls who are now office workers, nurses and teachers to go back to trapping and hunting in the bush? Or to sit in a tent and tan moose skins?

For young men, a few dollars can be made from trapping in the winter months, but this is only a stop-gap in the road to a man's economic independence. Generally he is wasting his time trapping when he could be reading and studying for a higher vocation.

Primary schooling is not only available to every child in the District of Mackenzie, but it is brought to every settlement at great cost to the Federal Government, not only in providing schools and living accommodation for teachers, but also in providing qualified teachers.

In its beginning, schooling for the North was fraught with many problems, but I believe no one today can deny the increasing success of the programme. In schooling at all levels the government has gone beyond making education free for all Northerners. Young Indian people are begged and cajoled into continuing secondary and vocational training. A great variety of fields are open to any who are willing to exhibit a modicum of effort in this direction.

Transportation costs are provided to and from the schools. All living expenses and costs of supplies and equipment for the courses are met by the government. On top of this a generous living allowance is given to each student enrolled.

The Department of Economic Development of the

Northwest Territories has budgeted for training and apprenticeship programmes for the fiscal year of 1976-77 the sum of $2,600,000. Of this amount approximately half is for the district of Mackenzie, with a population of about 26,000. The programme is open to all Northerners. About ninety-eight per cent of those selected for training are of Northern ancestry.

The Indian Brotherhood of the N.W.T., in a belligerent and narrow-minded way claim that the education programmes are meant for 'white' Northerners and do not fit the concept of education for the 'Indians' way of life.

If, in the North, there was no possiblity of developing any natural resources, either renewable or otherwise, and if the only way of life open for any of us was a life of hunting, trapping and fishing, then and then only would we be justified in withholding modern education from our young people and substituting a programme of teaching the arts of trapping and snaring beaver, tanning moose skins, making snowshoes, making babiche, sewing moccasins and paddling canoes. To deny the opportunities to our people of learning the skills to enable them to compete with other Canadians, is not only harmful, it is also stupid.

The right to full and free medical service is demanded. If we have not precisely that for everyone in the District of Mackenzie now, what *have* we got? As a matter of fact Indians get better consideration and service in this matter than do other residents of the N.W.T.. Not only are medical services and prescribed drugs offered free but in many cases government chartered aircraft will provide immediate transportation for the patient. Urgent and severe cases are flown to Yellowknife or to Edmonton, Alberta. Again, we have to thank the taxpayers of southern Canada for helping with these advanced facilities in the North.

9

LAND CLAIMS

The Indian Brotherhood argument seems to be that the land that was given up in Treaty Number Eleven was not in fact given up at all, and that the Indians of today must have this land back. The Indians want to be enabled to return to living in the lifestyle to which they were accustomed. It is the only way of life in which they can be happy and contented.

The Brotherhood spokesmen exhibit some fearful mental contortions in their desire to live two different lifestyles at the same time. They reiterate their longing and love for the lifestyle of the bygone days. Then in the same breath they want the wealth from Northern resource development to establish an industrial nation of their own.

Brotherhood spokesmen at the Berger Hearings keep repeating their claim to 'land' in general and seem to believe that if their words are repeated often enough their claims will gain in validity. Their spokesmen say: "...wherever the special relationship that aboriginal people have with the land has been disrupted..." and again, "...The land settlement of 450,000 square miles; that is our land,..." And still again from the Brotherhood submission, "In the process of building a pipeline, Native society would be dragged from a land based economy—hunting, fishing and trapping—into a wage economy, a wage economy which would be the poor Northern cousin of the southern economy..."

It seems obvious that the last quote was said with tongue in cheek. Southern people might imagine a majority of people of the North are engaged in hunting, trapping and shooting animals. The truth is that such a way of life is fast disappearing, and all Northerners know it. A wage economy is already here, and to be realistic wage economy offers the only hope for an increasing number of young people.

It would be useful if accurate comparative figures were available from the early part of the century showing the ratio of income from wild fur trapping to incomes from wage economy and to compare it with the situation today. Even now it is difficult to find definite figures showing just what percentage of income of Northern 'natives' is from trapping and what percentage is earned in the wage economy.

In the first part of the century it is likely ninety-eight per cent of the cash income of the native male population of the District of Mackenzie was from the sale or barter of wild furs. Possibly two per cent of the male adult natives were employed as interpreters in government service and for the trading companies. There were no other occupations available at that time for Northerners beside trapping. This was before the days of development and most people lived in the bush and part of their diet was from rabbits, moose, caribou and fish.

Statistics for the year 1972-73, show only one half of one per cent of the Indian and Metis population of the District of Mackenzie earned more than $1,000 from the sale of furs. This would leave about 3,000 male adults whose main income would have to be from the wage economy in one form or another.

There are today many Indian and Metis and others who supplement their wage income with week-end or part-time trapping. But a point to remember is that the total annual average sale of wild furs for the District of Mackenzie is only about $700,000. One set of figures from 1976 places the unemployment rate in some Northern settlements at forty per cent. The situation does not seem to have improved much since. The report also says the welfare payments for the Northwest Territories is about $1,800, compared with about $200 for the provinces.

The objective of Brotherhood propaganda is to convince southern Canadians that up to this time most Indians of the Mackenzie Basin were busily engaged in a hunting economy, and that they were happy and contented in roaming the great north woods. Now the bad white man comes along with his diabolical scheme to rip up the whole country with bulldozers, lay gas pipelines across their traplines, destroy and drive out the wild game and enslave the Indians in a wage economy. The solution to this catastrophe, they say, is to allow the Brotherhood to make a Dene nation of the District of Mackenzie, where with vast sums of money from royalties and land settlements, they will set up a government of their own. They infer that then the Indian people can go back to living their idyllic life. Conceivably, such a new nation would need an adminstrative and governing body. The royalties they speak of would be rolling in, and who better to spend it than the present Brotherhood leaders?

Since the Brotherhood was formed, many in the North could see this line of attack gradually taking shape. We said, "Surely, in this day and age such a tactic cannot succeed. Even southern Canadians will not be fooled." But when the newspapers and radio appeared to take up the refrain, we began to see that their scheming was having a degree of success. An occasional heroic soul who attempted to bring the truth to light was immediately branded as a 'racist' and was lined up with "Buffalo Bill" as an Indian-hater.

And when Justice Berger and the C.B.C. spokesmen appeared to swallow the bait and to accept the Brotherhood line, then I for one thought it time to speak up.

Another quotation from the opening statement of the Indian Brotherhood at the Berger Hearings declares: "Although the applicant (Canadian Arctic Gas) has filed with the Enquiry several thousand pages and millions of words covering a range of topics from perma-frost to interest rates, the total of its statement of the socio-economic impact of the pipeline consists of eleven pages. An examination of this so-called impact statement will reveal that the applicant's solicitude for the native people can be reduced to a simple, but hollow promise of jobs— a few hundred construction jobs which will disappear after the pipeline is built.....the hypocrisy behind the applicant's pious phrases is further revealed if we consider that, had the native people been consulted about the kind of jobs they wanted, pipeline jobs would have been far down the list. Development projects like this do not fit into the native system of priorities, and thus the jobs produced are really jobs for non-natives, imported from the south."

The hypocrisy mentioned above is, I believe, better fitted to the person making the charge. He must know that for the last twenty years, since the construction of the DEW line, the oil and gas exploration programmes of the North, the seismograph programmes, mining exploration and highway construction, the numbers of 'natives' continues to increase.

Indeed, it cannot be otherwise. The hire north programme alone trained hundreds of men and women as cooks, surveyors, chain saw operators, truck drivers, and heavy equipment operators. The general foremen of the right-of-way clearing camps were mostly Indian and Metis. And they did a very good job. Many young 'natives' through government sponsored programmes (costing a mint of money incidentally) are being trained today in many lines of vocational work: surveyors, electricians, carpenters, welders, cooks and bookkeepers. Arctic Gas is training many Northerners ('natives' if you will) not only to take part in the construction of the pipeline but also for maintenance crews for permanent jobs.

A land based economy for the District of Mackenzie would, if there were no wage economy jobs available at all, produce on the average about $250 for each family in the area. Let us see what the future offers in a wage economy, not forgetting that the fur crop can still be taken off as a part-time occupation.

Mr. Justice Berger mentioned the possibility of a corridor down the Mackenzie consisting of a gas pipeline, a highway, an oil pipeline, a railroad and a hydro electric transmission line. It is reasonable to assume that once a corridor is established, secondary industries will evolve and follow. A considerable number of people could be employed in catering to the tourist industry. There could certainly be manufacturing and fabricating of housing units. There will be a coal and mineral industry. There will always be surveying and road building, and as the population grows there is an agricultural potential in the Liard River Valley.

The Federal Government Experimental Farm at Fort Simpson, which was in operation for many years, proved that root crops and garden produce could be a viable industry, provided markets could be found within transportation limits. Much successful work has also been done on early-ripening grain crops. It is hardly conceivable that anyone would consider turning his back on the promising future which we have within our grasp, certainly not for a land-based economy which the Brotherhood spokesmen espouse so vehemently.

Running through the angry and often incoherent demands and accusation of the Indian Brotherhood, which now threatens to hold up development of the North, is an appeal to examine the hypotheses which they attempt to advance. This argument seems to run:

Indian people who have so recently emerged from the Stone Age cannot cope with the advancing western culture that is threatening to envelop them. Their old aboriginal way of life (they say) was a good way of life; it did not have the pressures, the temptations and the demands of our present society. The people had dignity and respect for one another and lived a relatively comfortable and peaceful existence. Thinking that they cannot cope with the present culture and its advancing technology, they wish to create a separate Dene nation, and imagine that they can build a wall around it and retreat into the past where they can resurrect the good old days.

Actually this option still exists today. Anybody in the North wishing to escape from 'white' society can simply move out of the settlements. He need go only a mile or so, and if he wants his primitive ways they are there.

People in the North occupy only a few tiny settlements and these needn't bother him if he wants to avoid them. The point is that nobody wants to turn his back on the amenities of society. So the Brotherhood's whole argument is fallacious and irresponsible.

Other advocates of 'native separatism', more realistically, say that in their own society, controlled by Indians only, with generous funding by Canada, Indians will be free from prejudice and interference from 'white men', and will in time modernize their nation and take their place in an advancing western society.

It seems to me that the outcome of a closed Dene nation might be the very opposite of that envisaged. At best it is wishful thinking to believe the Indians have the expertise to develop and direct an industrial nation, even if they were given the funding. Some of their spokesmen claim that they are now riddled with alcoholism, crime and family break-down. How would that change in their own society? The outcome of their envisaged scheme might not be the emergence from their Dene 'cocoon' as fully evolved members of an industrial society, but a degenerate copy of those who first withdrew behind the 'buckskin' curtain.

For by withdrawing from their fellow Northerners they will imply that they lack the confidence and the ability to take their place with other Northerners. Is it not possible that within the protection of the Dene 'cocoon' the process of retrogression might occur?

A great percentage of people in Canada and elsewhere dream at times of 'getting away from the rat race,' out into the backwoods, where they might live peacefully in a log cabin. They dream of throwing off the cares of the world and being happy and contented. Such people are predisposed to sympathy with the special relationship they believe the Indian to have to the land—the "old way of life." They do not see that this is practical neither for themselves nor for the Indian.

Such people overlook the fact that after a few weeks the solitude, the washboard, and the trek to the outhouse on a cold night lose their charm. The amenities of city life soon seem much more attractive. Ah, for the bathroom, the refrigerator, the gas furnace, the easy chair and the TV set!

The world is not so bad after all. But I see here in the paper tonight, *Indian spokesman says his people want to return to the land.* Sure, I'm all for it. If that's what they want, by all means let them do it. I'll believe it when I see it.

An Indian or a Metis or any other Northerner is exactly the same as you or I. We all like driving cars, dining out, bathrooms and gas furnaces—all modern conveniences. When will southerners learn that an Indian child at birth is not programmed to skin a muskrat, tan a hide or hunt and trap any more than a southerner is?

For the sake of argument let us assume that Indians of the District of Mackenzie want to go back to living in the bush. They will have to eat, so we'll assume they want to hunt and trap.

But the assumption will have to be corrected for even with every opportunity and assistance offered to trappers, most Northerners choose a life in the settlement where there is a chance of employment in the wage economy. But this means nothing to the Brotherhood. They persist in flying in the face of facts and keep screaming for 'land'. Fur and game are more plentiful, miles away from the Mackenzie River. They have been offered this land. But it seems that is not the land they desire. They prefer rights to the narrow strip along the Mackenzie River where the pipeline is to be built. That is where the towns will be: schools, liquor stores, supermarkets, airports, jobs, subsidized low rental housing, hospitals and doctors, welfare offices, roads and cars and all the exciting things that make up the good life. All these will be there if the pipeline is constructed.

One area in the controversy over land in the District of Mackenzie that should be cleared up is the right of any Northerner to own land as an individual. I think that there is general agreement in the North that an Indian should have equal rights to own, sell or occupy land, as all other Canadians have. It is the basic right of all Canadians to own and occupy land within our country, subject of course to our Federal and Provincial laws. In the N.W.T. today there is only one small Indian reserve, and it is within the boundary of the town of Hay River. *Aside from that one small area, there are no restrictions on the ownership of land within the Northwest Territories for any ethnic group. Indians and all others are equally subject to Federal and Territorial laws governing the ownership of land. So where is the problem?*

What the Brotherhood is concerned with here is *not* the legal right to own land, but their claim to the 160 acres or so of precisely that thread of the pipeline corridor.

All the talk about 'love for the land' is designed as a softening-up process for the land claims and relates to land given up under Treaty No. Eleven. The Brotherhood is asking for 450,000 square miles of land comprising the District of Mackenzie. They purport to wish to set up a Dene nation. What will this be but a gigantic Indian Reserve?

From the opening statement of the Brotherhood to the Berger Enquiry on March 3, 1975, their demands received a hearing. In referring to the claim of ownership of land, the statement in part read: "We also want to participate in Canadian society, but we want to participate as equals." Then again, "Only community ownership of the land which has belonged to our people for a thousand years can give us the ability to determine and follow our own way."

If this professed wish to participate in Canadian society as equals were sincere, they would not be opposing the creation of a Province of Mackenzie, where all Northerners would participate in a equal society.

On March 7th, 1975, a ten-page statement to the Berger Enquiry by James J. Wah-Shee of the Indian Brotherhood devoted considerable space to the land claims issue. He at first speaks of a claim to 400,000 square miles of land, and then later says that at a meeting in June, 1974, the Brotherhood upped the amount to 450,000 square miles. He says in part, "... that the only just and equitable land settlement is one based on land, not money."

The Brotherhood knows as well as anyone that the empty muskeg of the Mackenzie Valley is of little value by itself to anyone. What is at stake is the narrow strip, 1,000 feet wide, down the Mackenzie River. In an obvious jockeying for position, the Brotherhood could later say, "Sure, we are willing to compromise. We'll give up our claim to most of the 450,000 square miles, in return for 160 square miles comprising the Mackenzie corridor."

What they have been after all the time is complete control over the pipeline right-of-way. Through control, there will be royalties from the oil and gas, passing through the pipelines as well as rent and lease payments for the right-of-way.

Here is a rather astounding quote from the statement of Mr. Wah-Shee to the Berger Enquiry of March 7, 1975: "The evidence of two years of research, of taping the evidence of old people present at the signing of Treaties Eight and Eleven, and looking through historical files, indicated that *no mention of land surrender occurred* when the treaties were signed."

Here is what is written in Treaty No. 11, verbatim, from page six, third paragraph, "And whereas the said Commissioner has proceeded to negotiate a treaty with the Slave, Dogrib, Loucheu, Hare and other Indians inhabiting the district hereunder defined and described, which has been agreed upon and concluded by the respective bands at the dates mentioned hereunder, the said Indians do hereby cede, release, surrender and yield up to the government of the Dominion of Canada, for His Majesty the King and his successors for ever, all their rights, titles, and privileges whatsoever to the lands included within the following limits, that is to

106

say:

Commencing at the northwesterly corner of the territory ceded under the provisions of Treaty Number Eight; thence northeasterly along the height-of-land to the point where it intersects the boundary between the Yukon Territory and the Northwest Territories; thence northwesterly along the said boundary to the shore of the Arctic Ocean; thence easterly along the said shore to the mouth of the Coppermine River; thence southerly and southeasterly along the left bank of the said river to Lake Gras by way of Point Lake; thence along the southern shore of Lake Gras to a point situated northwest of the most western extremity of Aylmer Lake; thence along the southern shore of Aylmer Lake and following the right bank of the Lockhart River to Artillery Lake; thence along the western shore of Artillery Lake and following the right bank of the Lockhart River to the site of Old Fort Reliance where the said river enters Great Slave Lake, this being the northeastern corner of the territory ceded under the provisions of Treaty Number Eight; thence westerly along the northern boundary of the said territory so ceded to the point of commencement; comprising an area of approximately 372,000 square miles.

"And also, the said Indian rights, titles and privileges whatsoever to all other lands wherever situated in the Yukon Territory, the Northwest Territories or in any other portion of the Dominion of Canada."

How in the world could any sane and sober person stand in front of Mr. Justice Berger and say that there was no mention of land surrender in Treaty Number Eleven? Much of the treaty was in fact taken up with the land surrender by the Indians. The credibility of a person giving such a statement would be destroyed for ever, along with the credibility of the organization he represented.

10

SPEECH OF R.D. WARD

As Indian land claims has come to the forefront in the N.W.T. in the controversy over the building of the Mackenzie Valley pipeline, I here reprint a speech dealing with the subject by one of the most respected and best known Northerners, a man who has himself lived in the District of Mackenzie for many years. Even those who do not agree with his assessment of the subject of land claims will agree that there is not man in the North today who is more respected than Bob Ward for his knowledge of the area, his interest in all people, his honesty and integrity, his humanity and compassion, his good sense and practical mind.

"Notes from a speech by Robert D.S. Ward, Hay River, N.W.T.

"More learned people than I have spoken at length on matters relative to Land Claims and Native Sovereignty as it relates to the Northern part of Canada. I would first look at the literal meaning of the words as defined in the dictionary.

"The word 'Native' is defined in this matter, as being "one of a people inhabiting a Territorial area at the time of its discovery by a history-recording people.

"Eileen Jenness, in her book published in 1933, 'The Indian Tribes of Canada', indicates that the first inhabitants of North America emigrated from Asia, perhaps fifteen or twenty thousand years ago, gradually spreading south over parts of the North and South American continents as the centuries went by.

"Our recorded and written history indicates that when the first Europeans began their exploration of North America, there were, by a generous estimate, approximately 1,100,000 Indians on the whole continent. The great bulk of the continent was empty, and there were many places where large numbers were congregated, such as the Iroquois along the Mohawk River and the West Coast tribes of Canada. Inter-tribal warfare and massacres were common and kept the numbers limited.

"Again from Jenness where she speaks of the natives of the Mackenzie Valley. "Girl babies that were a burden to their mothers were often killed at birth; and the old and infirm were regularly abandoned to die of starvation and exposure." It was only after the white settlers penetrated the region that social, medical and economic improvements were made. The numbers of native people began to increase, and, of course, the inter-marriage of many early settlers and explorers with the native people helped to improve the stability of the Territory. Perhaps this will indicate the meaning of the word 'Native' as it applies and also that the numbers involved were few.

"It will be noted that the Indian Brotherhood has shown little trust for the written history of the white man, but prefer to accept a version of history as passed down by their elders by word of mouth. This, of course, is fraught with the dangers of poor and incomplete memories and interpretation to suit the situation.

"Now to sovereignty, which can be defined as the

110

supreme repository of power in a political state; independent; self-governing.

"We are also dealing with land claims, and I must say here that some of our historians were not too kind in their appraisal of Native Land Claims. Stephen Leacock, a noted historian, writing in his book, *Canada—The Foundation of its Future*, says, "We think of prehistoric North America as inhabited by Indians and have based on this a sort of recognition of ownership on their part. But this attitude is hardly warranted. The Indians were too few to count. Their use of the resources of the continent was scarcely more than the crows and wolves, their development of it nothing."

"Francis Parkman, in *Half Century of Conflict*, writes, "of Canada and its forested areas, lakes and rivers, the voyageur might wander for days without meeting, or expecting to meet, the face or trace of other human beings.

"Captain Butler in his book, *The Great Lone Land* (1870) wrote of our Northwest, "There is no other portion of the globe, in which travel is possible, where loneliness can be said to dwell so thoroughly. One may wander 500 miles in a straight line without seeing another human being.

"According to Leacock, "such and no more, is the meaning and extent of the Indian ownership of North America."

"On the other hand, we have the determined view of some people, mostly from southern Canada, I might add, that the whole of the Mackenzie District should become a sovereign state. Analogies were drawn with the emergence of the Native peoples of the third world, with reference to the colonization and exploitation. What was not mentioned is that some of the bloodiest massacres of all history have taken place when different factions within the emerging nations fight bitterly for power and control, *among themselves*, after withdrawl of the colonial power. Who is to say that the same may not occur here?

"We should also look at Treaties Number Eight and Number Eleven, wherein it states that not only should there be peace and goodwill, but also that, "the said Indians do hereby cede, release, surrender, and yield up to the government of Canada, all their rights, titles and privileges whatsoever to the land".

"Now, much has been made by publications and speeches from the Indian Brotherhood that these were only Peace Treaties. They choose to ignore the part of the Treaties relating to giving up the land. They also choose to ignore the fact that each time the treaties were discussed and formalized with a separate Band, there were Indian leaders present who signed on behalf of their people, as well as distinguished witnesses who signed the Treaties, declaring the same to have been read over, translated and explained to the Indians. Besides the government witnesses, we see prominently the names of Father Lacombe, Father Grouard, Bishop Breynat, and other priests and local citizens. Surely we don't expect that these good people, maliciously and with evil intent, misled the Indians, or would sign as witnesses if they were not content that the full meaning of the Treaties was not clear to all the Indians involved.

'I do not speak here as a representative of any group or organization, rather as an individual who has lived and worked in the North for over twenty years, and one who has a keen interest in the North and its people.

"I have discussed the matter at hand with a wide cross-section of the people of the North. There are radical views both ways on this question of Land Claims. Perhaps the middle ground is safer for all concerned. Owning land in Canada demands that we pay tax on our holdings. Undeveloped land is taxed the least, while highly developed property the most. We should keep this in mind. Canada cannot merely print money to meet the demands of her people for a variety of services provided. Taxes are one of the ways by which funds are raised.

"I would propose that clear title be given to all Indians, to that land within a community or settlement where they now live and have lived for some time, together with land set aside outside municipalities as a hunting preserve for each band where they traditionally hunt and trap. Band Councils could control the development of this land or leave it as is if so desired.

"The size of this land grant could be not less than one square mile per family as set out in the Treaties, with the borders set by establishment of local use, by members of the individual Bands. Each area and Band could negotiate the size and perimeter of such preserve. Insofar as sovereignty is concerned, the idea of a separate nation within Canada is unacceptable for many reasons, one which would be the terrible hardships that would be placed on the people within that nation if the government of Canada did withdraw. I feel that the aspirations of the Natives of the North are not really much different than those of others* who choose to live in the North.

*(In this context the word *others* is in reference to Government terminology; i.e. Indians, Eskimos, & Others, which we resent.)

"It seems to me that the best way to control our resources is through Provincial status: in other words, within the framework of the presently attainable democratic process. If this is not immediately attainable, then a time frame within which it will be attainable should be developed and people should prepare for that development.

"Meanwhile it is incumbent on the Government of Canada to (a) treat all residents as citizens of Canada with the same rights and responsibilities, and (b) set aside a portion of the Royalties from the exploitation of our natural resources in the form of a trust fund, to be turned over to us when Provincial status is obtained. That way, the new Northern Province could at least begin on a sound economic base.

"The native peoples, being in the majority, would have the dominant say in our new Province, through the duly elected representatives to that provincial government, and within our present democratic process. Any other way would lead to anarchy and chaos.

"When Newfoundland became a province, native Newfoundlanders dominated the provincial government, and do so to this day. We are lucky to live in this country, but we must remember that together with the benefits of oour society goes the terrible responsibility of donating to that society, not merely taking from it. Those who continually seek ways of taking from society will eventually destroy that society. It seems today that more and more people are speaking of division and special status. Stronger language is being used and this can only cause hardship and social unrest. Surely, responsible citizens should look for means to compromise without the use of inflammatory rhetoric.

"It has been written, 'However you shall sow, so shall you reap'. It is incumbent on the Government of Canada and the leaders of the Indian communities to sit down together and come to terms in settling the problems facing us. The British Common Law recognizes 'Squatters Rights' and that, together with the broad outlines of the Treaties and the generosity of the people of Canada, should resolve the problem. In summing up, Land Claims, yes, within limits, and as soon as possible. Native sovereignty, no. There is no place in this democratic nation for another government outside our present system, unless it is a government for all the people in the north, and by that, I mean provincial status."

11

THE JUST SOCIETY

As we read the outpourings of the leaders of the
Indian movement we must be encouraged and
heartened that Indians are standing up and being
heard. But I am saddened and disheartened by what
they are saying. They are right in bringing to light the
problems that exist, but the direction of their
solution, if adhered to, will spell doom for all those
who do not break out of the confines of the separate
areas being built for them.

Harold Cardinal in his book, *Unjust Society*, has
given an assessment of what he thinks the problems
are and, in some cases, his recommendations for
solutions. Most of his writing is taken up with
grievances against the government, modern society
and alleged 'white' suppression of Indians. Some
points are well made, and we must listen and reply
with honest answers.

He deals with government policies regarding
education among the Indians from the beginning
when the only formal education was in the hands of
missionaries. While this was better than no formal
education at all, much time was taken up with
instilling the Christian dogma and denominational
one-up-manship. Fortunately those days are prob-

ably gone for ever and formal education for all Canadians is gradually being separated from religious dogma. Cardinal then goes on to say that the government policy in education is to make little brown white men out of Indians. He is opposed to this and says his view of education for the Indians is to strike off the shackles of poverty and the tyranny of government direction.

The elimination of poverty in our country is analogous to the struggle against evil. We all agree on this objective, and it is not fair to accuse the Federal Government, by implying that there is some subtle quality in their education policies which perpetuate poverty among Indians.

The situation is much more complicated than that. My suggestion is that if the tangle of rhetoric, misconceptions, bigotry, and even honest mistakes of the past are cleared away, it will be revealed that the root of the problem lies in the fact that there *are* Indian Reserves. And as long as Reserves (with all their implications) exist, the people so confined will continue to struggle with a ball and chain.

Be that as it may, the writer then goes on to assume that the government has a devious and unscrupulous policy of assimilating and integrating Indian Canadians into our society. Let us hope that all policies are open and honest ones of assimilation and integration, and I cannot see anything un-scrupulous about it. It is the only practical solution.

We have no right in our false ego and pride to assign unborn millions to racial pigeon-holes where antagonism will be fostered more easily than in an integrated society. The welfare of the unborn generations should be our chief concern, rather than our hurt feelings and stubborn objectives of today.

Because of the rather comical friction and antagonism between the Christian sects as seen in the early days of the missionary schools the lack of understanding toward Indians and the incompetence of some teachers, the thought is expressed that today's education is all bad.

The truth is that the future of any group of people in Canada lies in getting into step with the changes and progress of today and the opportunities and challenges of the future. That is not to say that we should build more nuclear reactors and blindly go about wasting our resources and polluting the oceans. Progress lies in solving these problems.

What is a minority anyway? To some extent each one of us is in a minority in his beliefs, his attitudes and his style of living. In our country there is room for, and acceptance of, many minority opinions and styles of living. But we simply cannot exist as a nation unless we accept the concept that all of us must conform to the will of the majority. Such an hypothesis is the basis of a democratic society.

At the present time in Canada we are bending over backwards to accommodate 'minorities'. To have the 'clout' necessary to maintain themselves as a recognized minority they must have some strong feature which gives them cohesiveness. In the case of Indians of the District of Mackenzie any suggested cohesive features are illusive and transitory.

Let us examine a few—

1 Ancestry and color of skin—Through inter-marriage the cohesive factor here is fast disappearing.

2 Culture—This rather elusive word means many things to many people. By and large all Northerners will agree that Indians are clamouring to adopt western culture. It is unlikely that those who wish to retain their beaded jackets and head-bands can easily reject the style of life that so many are embracing with enthusiasm.

This doesn't mean that we must reject out of hand any features of any assimilated culture which will add to and enhance our own. A healthy culture is always changing to bring the greatest good to the greatest number of people. Neither should we embrace willy-nilly into our way of life new patterns which would weaken and destroy the cohesiveness we should try to maintain. The growth of society through selection, rejection and acceptance though frustrating at times, is a better way for a nation to go than to be cut up into a dozen separate entities.

3 Language—Mr. Justice Berger, speaking of the District of Mackenzie, says, "Four different races, speaking seven different languages." English is at this time the dominant language of the district. French of course is spoken by many Northerners also, as are 'native' dialects. This is not a disruptive force; quite the contrary. But the fact is that Indians are learning and speaking English and no one of the older native dialects is likely to be a cohesive force in maintaining a minority group.

12

BROTHERHOOD VIEWS

We should examine some of the views on the pipeline controversy, views from southern Canadians sympathetic to the Brotherhood viewpoint.

I will quote from the December 9, 1976, edition of *Newsletter* of the Committee for Justice and Liberty.

The *Newsletter* appears to be made up of the opinions and views of some Christian groups and churches. It is supported in part by Oxfam-Canada. Views and opinions on the pipeline and Northern development are quoted and explained in the *Newsletter*.

The organization of the CJL, they say, seeks to present an alternative vision and policies based on the Christian principles of justice, stewardship, love and compassion. They leave no doubt in their *Newsletter* of their position as anti-pipeline and pro-Brotherhood exponents. The inference is that if anyone dares to take an opposing view of pro-pipeline and anti-Brotherhood, it is tantamount to taking a position against Motherhood.

They imply that their supporters are good, pure and Godly. One who opposes their views must be wrong, and un-Godly. I, too, hold highly the virtues of justice, love and compassion, but I try not to let that make my thinking vacuous and wooly-headed. Informed reasoning, intelligence and courage will lead to solutions. Let us allow the discussion to be settled on the merits of the arguments advanced and not by inference of association, or theological dogma.

A quote from a leading article in the *Newsletter*, by John A. Althuis, speaking of the construction of the pipeline:

"Is it then a classic case of democratic 'trade-off'? A trade-off which requires a minority group of Northern Canadians to heroically abandon their desires for the sake of the greater public good so that southern Canadians and Americans won't freeze in the dark? Is it a case of North versus south, with the south destined to win because of its vast population and powerful position?"

Who says that the desires of the minority group are different from the majority of other Canadians? That is the crux of the whole controversy. Many Northerners today believe that the early construction of the pipeline corridor is in fact compatible with the desires and aspirations of the vast majority of the people in the Mackenzie Valley. More than this, I would also hazard a guess that the Brotherhood and their supporters would agree that the future of the people whom they purport to represent lies in the direction of development and industrialization of the North. Where they differ, I believe, is that the Brotherhood wants to have control of the funds accruing from development. My position is that a Northern Province of Mackenzie should have the control not only of funds from royalties but also control of the timing and direction of development through the democratic process to the same degree which the other provinces of Canada have.

The presumption advanced by some writers, that a small minority must give up their heartfelt ambitions because of the building of the pipeline, is erroneous and something I label as 'tripe'.

Mr. Althuis goes on to list the reasons why he thinks a moratorium should be established regarding the building of the pipeline.

"We need time to develop a National energy policy based on human growth values.

We need time to decide to switch to alternative renewable energy resources.

We need time to adopt to a much less energy intensive lifestyle.

We need time to begin the transition to a less capital and energy intensive production system.

We need time to restore our sick environment.

We need time to deal justly with our Northern neighbours.

We need time to reconsider our responsibilities to our Third and Fourth World neighbours.

We need a moratorium on the kind of Northern development that will lock us—and probably irreversibly so into a lifestyle that has already brought us such human and creational misery."

Is Mr. Althuis saying that he dislikes the lifestyle that he and others in southern Canada and the USA are living? If so he could easily move up to Northern Ontario, live in a log cabin, burn candles of whale fat, and carry his water from the creek.

We know that today the search is going on for alternative sources of energy. If there are answers to be found, we will find them. And if it does transpire that with the huge intellectual and technological resources at our command, we cannot find renewable resources for our energy demands, in, on, or near this planet, then we all of necessity will have to adjust our lifestyle in the meantime.

What right has Mr. Althuis to demand that in the meantime we in the Canadian North should sit and cool our heads, letting the oil and gas stay in the ground while you southerners go on living the good life, until a solution to the world's energy problems are solved? In the North the young people coming out of school are swelling the ranks of the unemployed, and there is no room in the south for them. The south cannot employ its own. Are we to tell them to go back to the trapline and live on bannock and rabbits? Have they to submit to a lower standard of living than you in the south, while we wait till you say 'Go'?

And as to restoring the 'sick environment', why not restore your own in the south? We will look after our own here in the future Province of Mackenzie.

The next article in the *Newsletter* of CJL is titled "Of Pipelines, Peacepipes, & Buried Promises" and is prepared by David T. Steen. It goes like this:

"As Staff Coordinators for project North an interfaith group formed by the efforts of Roman Catholic, Anglican and United Churches, the McCullums have researched and travelled extensively through the North. After years of work, their findings can be summed up as follows: Everywhere we have gone in the Northwest Territories the same refrain is heard. "The pipeline will destroy us (Native Peoples) unless our land and our rights are safeguarded". Project North then is attempting to act as a buffer so that Native people in the North achieve a just settlement of their land claims before further resource development prejudices their claims. Once the pipeline is completed, the damage to the style of life among the native people will have been done. There will be nothing left to negotiate. A way of life will be threatened with extinction."

Another quote from the McCullums. "The closest definition we can come to is that, for the Natives, land is for use: it is like a Mother. It is a breadbasket, protector and friend. It has always been there and will always be there. And out of it comes your being, the reason for your existence, the only power you have in the white man's world. If you lose it or sell it or have it taken away from you, then you are dead, or at best a second class white man."

So that was the refrain they heard wherever they went in the Northwest Territories? Well, well. I suppose that you hear what you want to hear and believe what you want to believe. But it is extremely odd that these two investigators did not see that there are but few people in the North today who are truly 'living off the land'. In truth, how could they? The only cash crop of the land is wild fur. The average annual crop of fur in the Northwest Territories is $1,400,000. If half is taken in the Mackenzie District that would be $700,000 or about $220 per family per year. Supplemented with meat and fish (and that supply is very limited) they would make a very poor living indeed.

In the opposite direction of education and resource development lies hope. During and after the construction of the corridor, there will remain 449,840 square miles of the 450,000 square miles of the District of Mackenzie that will be wide open and where the Brotherhood can settle, unmolested in their Mother land, their breadbasket, their protector and friend, where they will not have to become second class white men.

Why are the churches lending their voice to these words which seem so patently dishonest? Are they blinded by mistaken compassion for a people whom they consider to be hopelessly inadequate in their ability to enter into the modern world? Are they so certain that the natural resources of the North should be saved for a rainy day that they believe the means they use in this case will justify the end?

At any rate, the Committee for Justice and Liberty Foundation are concerned with slowing down the rate of consumption of our non-renewable energy resources and the corresponding search for renewable energy sources and the adoption of a much less energy intensive lifestyle.

If that assessment is correct then who will say them nay? But let us be objective about it. Northern Canadians cannot do it alone.

It will take a concerted effort over the entire continent to swing the trend away from our present lifestyle. Most people in our society will not give up driving their cars, or heating their homes, or travelling and using up energy in numerous ways. We all say we want others to conserve energy while we continue our mad pace.

The point here is that whatever the opinion of Canadians may be regarding the broad subject of the conservation of energy it is pathetic to see the CJL embracing the cause of the Indian Brotherhood in order to strengthen their position on energy problems.

Just suppose for a minute that the National Energy Board does put a ten-year moratorium on the construction of the pipeline. What will happen to the literally thousands of people of the Mackenzie Valley who will enter the labour force in that time? The Brotherhood might get a big chunk of land in their settlement in the meantime. But will they get the millions in cash they are asking for? It seems doubtful. What 'Native' projects could they possibly set up that would employ the expanding population, without going to resource development?

.The land grant they receive is not likely to be the 450,000 square miles of the District of Mackenzie they are asking for. But whatever they get will inevitably be termed a 'Reserve', which is a retrograde step in itself. Just who will be confined to this area? Who will decide on who or what is a 'native'?

There are now about 4,500 Metis in the Mackenzie Valley and in ten years' time there could be twice that number. Many of them are white skinned. Can they all be lumped into a 'native' basket? What about Northerners like myself? I could argue that by the dictionary definition I am a native Canadian. Would I be left out of the settlement? What about the people who honestly wish to consider themselves as 'Natives', and others who are dumped into the basket?

Headlines will scream at them from all directions, and for many years, "You are Indians. You are aborigines. We are setting you apart from the rest of Canada because you are a separate race, a different people from other old Canadians as well as new Canadians. We imply that you are somehow inferior in that you need special treatment and consideration. Some of you leaders say that you cannot compete in our society, so we are fencing you off where, we are told, you will be safe from detrimental effects of progress."

If we as Canadians do this thing to other Canadians merely because of their ancestry, it will show that as a people we are totally insensitive.

And please do not say they will do all right in their own society, that they will remain segregated and with money from oil and gas royalties from the North they will find employment for all and in time will catch up with the rest of us. If they are put on a reserve it will still be impossible for them to remain segregated. In Northern Canada the movement of people is accelerating with the network of roads and airports. The rate of intermarriage is increasing and there are many Indians and Metis (and Eskimos) who will not be set back for ten years in what will amount to a ghetto. Those who can, will break out. Will they be welcomed as fellow Canadians? Or will they be sent back to their own 'country'?

What a caldron of sadness and grief we set upon the fire for ourselves if we allow this to happen.

Before we leave the McCullums and the article by David T. Steen, I must say something about their comment on how they think the 'Native' regards the land. "It is like a Mother. It has always been there. Out of it comes your being, the only power you have in the white man's world....."

This is loose and shallow rhetoric. Do not these statements seem familiar? We read about Mother Nature in Grade One. Does anyone not love his native land?

And what about, "Out of it comes your being, the only power you have in the white man's world.....? This seems to imply that the land claims the leaders and advisers are always talking about is the only lever they have to wrest from the Federal Government a sum of money sufficient to live and grow fat on for the rest of their lives.

Is the talk about living on the land sincere? The leaders who make these statements living in hotels, travel on jet aircraft, drive cars, eat the best food, visit the doctor as necessary (free Medicare) and seem to enjoy the so-called detested modern society. Would they not like to continue in that life style?

Again in the *Newsletter* of the Committee for Justice and Liberty is an article prepared by Stanley W. Carlson. The sub-heading is, "A digest of the evidence of Melville Watkins. Melville Watkins is Professor of Economics, University College, University of Toronto. He served as the economic consultant to the Indian Brotherhood of the Northwest Territories from 1974 to 1976."

Watkins takes the view that building the Mackenzie pipeline and the later extraction of resources will be for the 'public interest' and will not promote 'genuine development' for the Native people. He speaks of the 'plight' of the Native people of the region and says that the smooth talk of 'the greater good' and the 'national interest' conceals the perpetuation of long term Canadian maltreatment of those of its people who were the original inhabitants of the land. Watkins says the Natives have been forced to make the traumatic shift from being 'land-bound' men to becoming 'industrial men' under the condition of forced industrialization. He says 'forced' is not too harsh a word when he speaks of the process by which land-bound man is turned, against his will, into industrial man and thus integrated into the market of 'modern' economy.

If Mr. Carlson's summary of the 'evidence' given by Professor Watkins is fair and true, then the time Watkins spent in giving this evidence could have been better utilized in a game of tiddly-winks with Justice Thomas Berger.

Professor Watkins is pre-supposing conditions in the North which do not exsist today, and also seems to be guilty of some dissembling in order to make his point. He imagines that the former 'land-bound' life of natives was a good way of life that was upset when the fur traders and settlers arrived. He ignores what a slight bit of thought and investigation would show, that their Stone Age existence was hardly a way of life for beasts of the field. Then he suggests that the transition can be made to a modern way of life if 'Natives' have control over development. He deliberately ignores the fact that there are many other people involved in the economic future of the North aside from those he terms 'Natives'. Government figures for population in the Mackenzie Basin give these numbers: Indian and Eskimo, 11,000; Metis and others 14,500. It is dishonest to ignore the fact that there are many Northerners who cannot honestly be termed Indian or Eskimo. Then Watkins goes on to imply that all 'natives' wish to go his way.

We would be wise to temper our idealism with realism. Possibly we can learn something from the past, but let us not live in the past. We must be cognizant of conditions, attitudes and desires of the people of the North today. We should be fully aware of what is happening in the North today before we offer suggestions for the future.

Allow me to lay to rest the old 'bogey' of talk of

degradation of 'Natives' of the North. Opponents of the construction of the pipeline often use the words degradation, prejudice and exploitation, when they refer to any Northerners but 'whites'. 'Prejudice' toward Northerners of any extraction has previously been covered in this essay. And if there is any exploitation of people in regard to Northern development, it is the Federal Government who are exploiting the Canadian *taxpayer* for the benefit of Northerners and especially the Indians.

But what about the 'degradation' that 'whites' are accused of subjecting Indians to? The word 'degrade' implies the action of someone to lessen the state, position or status of someone else. The Indian Brotherhood is attempting to degrade other Northerners, both 'white' and Indian, who want an egalitarian society of the North, as opposed to the Brotherhood's Dene society.

The government certainly is not trying to 'degrade' natives. Quite the contrary. Anyone who is truthful and honest in his assessment will acknowledge that there is a tremendous effort by the N.W.T. Administration to improve the conditions, opportunities and status of those Northerners who are at the bottom of the economic ladder. But then someone says, "How about those who spend their time in the pubs of the North drinking themselves into oblivion and allowing their family life to deteriorate? And is not the 'white' culture encroaching upon the natives to blame for that?"

I would answer that anyone who is foolish enough to behave in that manner is doing so of his own free will. They are not being forced into it any more than the throngs of people on the 'outside' world who do the same.

Our present society does demand more sophisticated patterns of behaviour than did a Stone Age culture, but most people, including Northerners, believe that the benefits of our present society outweigh the disadvantages. People are swarming to our cities (the centres of our culture). I do not notice any noteworthy movement of people back to the bush. Professor Watkins speaks of the natives wanting to create an 'egalitarian' society. The word must have been a slip of the tongue, for 'egalitarian' is a belief in a society of equals. The Brotherhood does not want equality. They want special status and privileges. Otherwise they would be happy with provincial status for the Mackenzie District and a dynamic development programme, where we would have a true egalitarian society.

Watkins seems to think that a 'land-bound' existence has merit. Many 'natives' in the North do not seem to think so. The increasing numbers of young people leaving school and seeking work in the wage economy are not clamouring to go back to the bush. They obviously do not have a desire for a 'land-bound' life and are, in fact, determined on a modern industrialized way of life.

Watkins refers also of the 'plight' of the 'native' people in the District of Mackenzie who make up somewhat less than half the population of that area. I, in turn, speak of the 'plight' of *all* Northerners in our area. And by 'plight' I mean the present situation in which 'white' sentimentalists from 'Outside' are helping reactionary elements in the North to retard progress. We believe that construction of the Mackenzie corridor will lead to a development of the North which will stem from exploitation of our resources and not from exploitation of the people.

It is suggested that the creation of an eleventh province is impractical and unlikely. I would reply that a Province of Mackenzie is far more logical and consistent with out political institution than is a separate 'Dene' nation.

Professor Watkins speaks of schools which destroy indigenous Dene skills. I somehow doubt if there is such a thing as 'indigenous skills.' I would think that skills are mainly acquired, except in rare cases of artists or musicians. And possibly the right words in that case would be an aptitude for developing certain skills. For most of us, Dene or otherwise, skills must be learned, and our government is now bent on teaching the skills of the modern world to the young people of the North. There are also many programmes of adult education and vocational training.

There are at the present time a small number of exceptional people in the North whose skills that have survived their practical use, are now of great value as arts and crafts. These include carving, moose hide and caribou hide bead and silk work, moose hair work, and the making of small birchbark containers and snowshoes. Possibly, Watkins is referring to these when he speaks of indigenous skills. The government of the Northwest Territories have funded and encouraged Co-ops and retail outlets for such products. We believe that, with development, the tourist trade will expand and the market for handicrafts of many kinds should increase. But, at best, this industry will employ but a small number of the labour force. To envisage all Dene employed in these 'indigenous skills' is preposterous.

Professor Watkins speaks of over-riding the 'Native' interest. Surely it is presumptuous or worse for a southern Canadian to assume that people who live in the North have different interests, aspirations and ambitions from southern Canadians.

If there is to be sensible and intelligent development of the North, then all will benefit. If on the other hand a ten-year moratorium is established on the construction of the pipeline, then all Northerners will suffer in consequence.

Watkins says, "The task of restructuring the Canadian economy is long overdue." Perhaps. But

134

the economic structure of our country will change
and evolve as the majority of people see fit, and as
pressures are built up. It is unfair to expect Northerners to sit in teepees in the bush waiting for society
to be restructured.

Watkins continues..."and the need for a humane
approach to Northern development is the best
possible reason for beginnning now. To respect the
Native interest will be to serve the true public
interest."

If by native he means all Northerners, then we
must agree. And if in the following, he means all
Northern people when he refers to Natives, then I
think few Northerners would disagree.

He says, "We have every reason to expect that the
true public interest can be better served by the
Native peoples—as long term residents with a
heritage of respect for the land, because they are the
closest to the area to be so affected."

13

ENVIRONMENTAL DAMAGE

Twenty years ago many people had never heard of the word 'ecology', and the word 'environment' was used mainly in reference to the surroundings of a virus or bacteria. But in the last few years both words have come into common usage. There are few in the advanced nations of our planet Earth who are not aware of the importance of the physical aspects of our surroundings to the survival of man. Together with the physical aspects of our planet, we couple the rather intangible psychological factors which affect us, and use the term 'environment'. It is *the* word of today.

Much has been said about the dangers to wildlife stemming from the contemplated construction of the Mackenzie pipeline corridor. There have been different views to the seriousness and degree of harm to the birds, mammals and fish of the area. Some of those who oppose building the pipeline have been prophets of doom and gloom in predicting terrifying consequences on caribou, muskrats, marten, fox, fish and birds.

In 1943 the Canol Pipeline and road were built from Norman Wells near the Arctic Circle, on the Mackenzie River, across the mountains to the Yukon and Alaska. Damage to the terrain and wildlife of the area was about as much as the ocean would be affected by a shower of rain. There were piles of junk from the construction left here and there, but that need not happen again.

It is simply not true that the projected corridor would destroy any appreciable amount of wildlife. It is not roads, with the noise from vehicles, that harm wildlife. Timber wolves and man with his high-powered rifles are the danger.

Access to hunting areas recently by way of skidoo, for instance, has forced us to realize that outdated all-year-round hunting rights by residents must be reviewed. We have already discussed the recent problems created by the swift depletion of the Alaska caribou herds.

Some, in opposition to the pipeline, try to maintain that the pipeline corridor area is significant to the overall supply of wilderness area in the Northwest Territories.

The following words appear in a report on the Berger Enquiry. "It appeared at the Enquiry that there was general agreement that wilderness (land in the natural state) was in limited and decreasing supply."

Is this quote meant for people who are half asleep or thick in the head? No one believes that land or wilderness area is infinite; therefore, it certainly must be limited. Is wilderness area decreasing, or likely to decrease to any noteworthy extent by the construction of the pipeline? In the ten Canadian provinces there might be reason for concern of wilderness depletion. That matter concerns the provinces. But in the Northwest Territories, the pipeline will encroach upon a very small fraction of wilderness area. If the corridor is 1,000 feet wide (room for 5 right-of-ways) the area taken up will be approximately .03 per cent of the area of the District of Mackenzie. (160 square miles out of 450,000 square miles).

Wildlife, some are also suggesting, will be endangered by more frequent flights of aircraft over the are. Again, during the Berger Enquiry, someone recommended that aircraft should fly at a minimum height of 2,500 feet above ground, to avoid disturbing wildlife and suggested an agency should designate specific flight corridors during all seasons. It is implied there should be strict regulations governing the operation of all aircraft in the N.W.T. to reduce the hazard to wildlife.

In regard to the low flight of fixed-wing aircraft in relation to moose, caribou, bear, fox and lynx in wilderness areas, I know from personal experience that these animals soon become accustomed to the sound and the sight of aircraft flying low. When on floats, you can taxi right up to them, get out and tie up your aircraft without alarming them to any great extent.

Moose, for instance, while feeding, will approach the moored machine to within 50 feet. Lynx, fox and black bears will run off 100 yards or so and watch through the bushes. This state of affairs applies only if the animals are never shot at or molested.

Most wild animals will even get accustomed to helicopters working in the vicinity, provided the pilot uses common sense in his manoeuvering and does not deliberately 'buzz' the animals. There are first-hand reports of grizzly bears being 'shot' with tranquilizer guns at close range by biologists wishing to measure and study them. After being subjected to these 'attacks' several times, the bears turn belligerent and come charging when the helicopter approaches.

This practise must be stopped before an ugly incident occurs and someone besides the bear gets hurt. In a rare case when a mentally disturbed grizzly runs amock he should be immediately destroyed, but otherwise the animals should be left strictly alone. They seem to be creatures with unique personalities, and can develop a monumental 'grouch' when harassed.

Ordinarily, and with the exception of grizzly bears, animals in the wild will soon learn to live on friendly terms with noisy vehicles of all kinds. If completely ignored they soon learn to go about their own affairs when it is evident they are not in danger. More than once I have landed a float-equipped aircraft on a mountain lake and touched down within 100 feet of a moose that went on feeding and hardly looked up at me. Caribou are curious and will often run up to you and then dash away. Lynx will sit on the side of the road and watch trucks go roaring by; they seem to be intrigued by the rumbling monster.

The whole secret is—leave the animals and birds alone and it is surprising how soon they will come to trust you.

Even amongst the Dall mountain sheep of the Mackenzie Mountains the tendency to become friendly with man is marked.

There was a case in the Nahanni mountains where a pilot landed near the top of a mountain at about 5,000 feet elevation. During several days when he flew back and forth establishing a tent camp, he often noticed a herd of six white rams, grazing within a stone's throw. The aircraft roaring in and out on the landings and take-offs scarcely bothered them.

In the construction of the pipeline, if pilots of aircraft can be induced to use a little common sense, then legislation to control the height, direction and speed and noise of aircraft will be superfluous. If, on the other hand, there is legislation to prevent aircraft from flying low, there will inevitably be accidents and people will be killed if the regulations are not enforced. Much of the time when flying VFR, a pilot must fly low in following valleys in mountainous terrain, when there is a low ceiling as is often the case. Even if both he and his aircraft were IFR equipped, he cannot enter the clouds, switch from VFR to IFR and fly safely.

In view of the concern expressed over environmental damage from the construction of the pipeline, a vast amount of time, energy and money has been spent on research in this area.

In the last four years Canadian Arctic Gas alone has spent more than $16 million in studies of northern wildlife and vegetation, employing up to fifty professional field researchers. This information, and much more, is available to the Federal Government and will no doubt be used when rules and regulations for the building of the pipeline are handed down.

In regard to environmental studies generally in the North, there is a further point that deserves serious attention.

The degeneration of the quality of our ocean water from oil spills and garbage from sewers, the pollution of our fresh water streams and lakes, pollution of the air and to some extent land, with chemicals, insecticides and herbicides, is likely the biggest danger that mankind has ever faced. Surely these dangers cannot be over-emphasized. There are, of course, other dangers to the environment, which are of lesser consequence. Let us keep the dangers to our environment in proper perspective.

To placate the southern Canadian voters, we allow or demand a study of the magnitude mentioned in the District of Mackenzie. At the same time, and right before our eyes, pollution of the oceans is taking place at a rate which, if continued, could choke off our oxygen supply before we burn one cubic foot of gas from the pipeline.

We must not forget, when we think of the pipeline and wildlife of the area, that there is a conflict between so-called 'native hunting rights' and the supply of wildlife especially caribou, which has been demanding attention since the advent of the high powered rifle and, latterly, the advent of the skidoo and outboard motors.

Violence to gain political ends—There have been both overt and implied threats of violence reported in the press by spokesmen for the Council of Yukon Indians and the N.W.T. Indian Brotherhood. To my knowledge, no one for the Federal government has reacted with a public statement regarding the threats. The failure to warn against such foolish talk warrants criticism. I am shocked and disgusted when a man is allowed to stand before a Royal Commission, and give vent to such words as: "As long as the Dene blood flows in this land, this pipeline will be built only with our consent, or it will flow red to the south," Raymond Yakelaya told the Berger Hearings in Norman Wells.

Freedom of speech is one thing. Threats of violence before a public hearing, chaired by a Judge, are another matter.

Many people feel that the pipeline will be built, no matter what Mr. Yakelaya says, and if there is blood spilled in consequence thereof, I submit that others than Mr. Yakelaya should share the blame.

Teachers, historians and philosophers, I am sure, all agree that violent reaction by any group of people against another group is morally justified only in extreme cases of cruel treatment, oppression and torture, and where there is no possibility of redress through the courts of law.

Do I hear some Brotherhood spokesmen say, "That's me. That's me. We have suffered from oppression, insults, arrogance, discrimination and prejudice from the 'whites' for far too long. Therefore we are justified in using violence to gain our ends."

I would reply, "You wouldn't be using the threat of violence as a lever to get a larger slice of pie from a settlement with the authorities, with the help of publicity generated by press coverage of the Berger Hearings?"

Violence to Crown property, or the threat of violence, can only harm us all. We live in one of the most enlightened and progressive countries in the world where we do have freedom of speech. Use it. Stand up and be counted and say what is in your mind, but for God's sake (and your own) do not listen to those who advocate violence. One might think that our government is soft and easy-going, but I am assured that they will not tolerate violence against the Crown.

Another reason why I am ashamed of the threats which have been publicized in the coverage of the Berger Hearings is that the state of mind thus exhibited by some individuals is not shared by ninety-eight per cent of Northerners of whatever ancestry. Southern Canadians might get the impression that many of us in the North have sympathy for such irresponsible talk. This is not the case. Indians in the District of Mackenzie deplore the thought of violence against the Crown, or against another human being.

14

SUMMING-UP

The path we will take in the North must offer the best possible future for all Northerners. There must be opportunity for all. We should give some consideration not only to ourselves and our children, but to the broad environment into which Northerners yet unborn will enter.

At the same time we must not forget that we are part of a nation and the interest of all Canadians must be taken into consideration.

The Indian Brotherhood is taking a selfish and unrealistic line of approach when they demand control of the District of Mackenzie and a huge cash settlement for their so-called 'aboriginal' land rights. It is selfish because it excludes many other Northerners from taking part in the development of what is as much theirs as the Brotherhood's. It is unrealistic because the demands are for untold wealth in return for absolutely nothing. To lay claim to the whole of the District of Mackenzie is nothing less than preposterous. For many years the Federal Government has been pumping millions of dollars into the Northwest Territories for the betterment of conditions and opportunities for every man, woman and child. Sixteen million dollars have been given to the Brotherhood and other so-called 'native' organizations for propaganda, research and administration of these organizations.

Wealth is not something that grows on trees. Our country's wealth is produced by Canadians working with hand and brain. Is it going to be pumped into some bottomless pit because of the guilt complex of a few Canadians?

The demands are unrealistic because they are far too large. It is fallacious to assume any government in its senses would accede to them. Perhaps exaggerated demands are thought to give a better bargaining position, but it could possibly weaken the credibility of the position taken when other matters are discussed.

In regard to the so-called 'land claims', the square mile of land, under Treaty Number Eleven, awarded to each family should be undeveloped land. Provisions could be made for the exchange, at the wish of the individuals concerned, for a smaller parcel of developed land. (A serviced lot within a settlement.) A family should not have to accept a parcel of land in a 'ghetto' in any community. Free choice as to where he would like to live would be a manifestation of his equality with other Northerners. Indians in the District of Mackenzie own and operate businesses, separately and in groups. They also have the right to own land as individuals.

We should be very careful that any community ownership of land by Northerners would not fall into the category of a 'Reserve'. Indian Reserves are a malignant growth in the body of Canada. There must be an early diagnosis and removal. They are today completely outdated. The concept of Reserves cannot fit into our advancing ideas of freedom and equality. It will no doubt be painful to remove the Reserves but Canada will be healthier without them.

The consequences of setting a large group of people aside from a competitive society by maintaining them in affluence for any length of time by acceding to huge demands, will damage them extensively and leave scars which will take generations to heal.

Today many men and women of so-called 'native' blood are doing well in fitting themselves into a changing economy and lifestyle. Any honest person living in the District of Mackenzie, who has been observant, will surely agree. It is equally true that many are not yet making the effort necessary to adjust. If we provide the opportunity and fair conditions they must be capable of contributing the effort.

Analogies are not always true in the duplication of a situation, but I will venture one here. We Northerners are presently engaged in what amounts to climbing a long, steep hill. The snow is deep and the weather is cold. Some have already made it to the top. Others are struggling manfully and making progress. Others have given up, have removed a bottle from their pockets and are sitting back, shedding tears. Instead of carrying them to the top of the hill on a free chair lift, (built especially for them at great expense) would it not be wiser to offer them better equipment and a helping hand to get started again? Then, when they do reach the top, they can say, "I am up here with the rest, and I did it without having to be carried."

In short, if the demands of the Brotherhood are met in full, many people of 'native' ancestry will be set back for many years and perhaps never regain their confidence, pride and determination to carry on. Children born into their society will feel that because they are born 'Indians' they are somehow not quite real people and are destined to be denied a chance, while the rest of the world passes them by.

Having come so far in the struggle to have

Northerners accepted as equals with other Canadians, and just now when 'natives' are showing that they have the ability to learn the skills of the modern age, why should we, at precisely this time, contemplate 'throwing in the towel'? If we do, we will be guilty of a clear example of misdirected compassion.

All through the essay I have implied that there is an alternative programme for the North other than that advanced by the Brotherhood. This alternative programme is largely in keeping with government programmes already dealing with the North. It is a programme in line with the thoughts expressed by many Northerners of 'native' ancestry, as well as most who were originally from other parts of Canada. Central to this programme is the view that the settling of legitimate land claims should not hold up the construction of the Mackenzie Valley Pipeline. It is the responsibility of the Federal government to work out a satisfactory settlement with the concerned parties, and the sooner the better.

After having read Treaty Number Eleven, negotiated with the Mackenzie District Indians and signed by them in June, July, August of 1921, and the Liard Band in August of 1922, I would suggest that they have received far more in benefits than they could reasonably have expected with full Canadian citizenship.

The belief is general among most Canadians that the Mackenzie Valley gas pipeline will be built if the supply of gas warrants the expenditure. The question which Northerners might be able to influence in some small way, is when the pipeline should be started.

Industrial development in the North is of the utmost importance to us all. A ten-year moratorium on the pipeline would have devastating social consequence. With 40% unemployment rate in some of the northern settlements we must extend every effort to decrease the unemployment not to increase it. A Northern settlement of fewer than 1,200 people right now, which has seven members of the R.C.M.P. to maintain law and order, and requiring the services of three Justices of the Peace, with a visiting Magistrate or Judge, is to my mind a deplorable situation. More idle, unemployed people would surely extend this problem.

For this reason alone we should not hesitate in getting started on the pipeline. If and when the Federal Government is satisfied that the successful applicant has the funds and the technical knowledge to build a pipeline, and if the known supply and potential of natural gas justifies it, then we should start immediately to plan for the construction of a 'corridor'.

All manpower and industry should be mobilized immediately to finish the road which is now partially constructed to the Mackenzie River delta. It seems that this road was envisioned as long as six years ago by the Department of Northern Affairs, and possibly 100 miles of it has already been constructed. The work force of the N.W.T. is increasing at approximately 1,000 persons a year.

During construction of the road, supply depots of pilings, lumber, cement, fuel and other non-perishable supplies should be set up at appropriate sites. With river barging on the Mackenzie River and winter and summer surface transportation, this work could continue throughout the year. The corridor right-of-way with the highway could be completed within two years. During that time many additional Northerners might be trained to help with the actual construction of the pipeline.

All organizations within the Northwest Territories that have an interest in the development of the North, or the impact of such, should, together with the government of the N.W.T., set up a governing body, funded by the government, to coordinate all work programmes. The object of this governing body would be to see that employment of Northerners be as complete as possible and that damage to the people and the terrain would be minimal.

We would suggest that the proposed Development Coordination Board be set up in Yellowknife, with power, through the Commissioner of the N.W.T., to enforce their decisions. The Board should be composed of mobile field officers, representatives from Band Councils, Settlement Councils, Metis Organization, Non-Status Indians, The Indian Brotherhood, Chamber of Commerce, Department of Social Development, Department of Economic Development, Manpower and the Canadian Wildlife Service.

If one sensible environmentalist could be found, he should be included on the Board. The Board must have power and must be responsible to the Legislative Assembly of the Northwest Territories.

The Development Coordination Board, thus set up, would continue to oversee the actual construction of the pipeline and all other construction within the corridor, with the same objectives in view, as during the preliminary work of the construction of the Mackenzie highway.

After the preliminary work has been done, and the Development Coordination Board has been satisfied that all is in readiness, then the actual work of the laying of the pipeline could begin. Now, representatives of the consortium who are the builders of the pipeline should be brought into the Development Coordination Board.

With all the information that has been gathered relating to the environmental and social impact of the construction of the corridor, and with the cooperation of the people through the Development Coordination Board, we should not expect any shattering damage in and around the construction area.

Some will say that a suggested Dene nation could handle the development in a way that would be more satisfactory to the 'natives'.

One consideration would be that the Indian Brotherhood admit that they aren't interested in non-Indians which, including the Metis, make up a majority of the population of the District of Mackenzie.

There have been charges made that development destroys the 'native' way of life through alcohol and welfare abuse. Would alcohol problems be fewer in a Dene nation than in an anticipated Province of Mackenzie?

And how about 'welfare'? Under a Dene government, would The Brotherhood turn the old, the sick, and the lame out into the cold to die, as was done in the Indian Stone Age? Or would they receive welfare?

Fear has been expressed that with industrial development of the North, some people will be dragged from the 'traditional' way of life in which they wish to remain. A close assessment of the matter will show that with the expansion of the wage economy, more people will in fact be enabled to live in the bush to trap and hunt if they wish. To live in the bush nowadays takes money: for skidoos, boats, motors, traps, tents and such. With money earned from wages more people will have a chance to live at least part time in the bush.

There will likely be criticism directed against the concept of a Province of Mackenzie with equality for all citizens. It will be said that Indians will still be dominated by the 'white man'. Under provincial status any ethnic political domination seems unlikely. The legislature will be subject to democratic majority vote. With free speech and equal opportunity we should be on our way to a truly egalitarian society.

Some of those advocating a ten-year moratorium on the building of the pipeline deplore the change from the old way of life. How old do they mean? Are they referring to the days before the first fur traders and settlers arrived? Are they suggesting that a Stone Age existence had many advantages over the present day? If by 'the old way of life' they mean the days soon after steel knives, axes, guns, tents and blankets were introduced by the 'white' man, then I will agree that there were some advantages to living then. But it is unrealistic to imagine that we could live that way for ever.

The Indian Brotherhood advocates a separate Dene nation where Indians will establish their own government. The implications of this country being divided into separate nation states on a racial basis is frightening. Such a line of reasoning implies that Indians are not capable of deciding their own destiny within the framework of a Province of Mackenzie. I am left with the impression that the Brotherhood leaders regard Indians as aborigines, inferior citizens, who cannot compete on equal terms with others. They apparently wish to fence themselves off from all the evils of a 'white' dominated society.

In the pluralistic society of the North which I envisage, in a climate where pride and confidence will be nourished in all young people, there will at least be a fighting chance for everyone to reach whatever potential has been inherited at birth. In a closed Dene society, on the contrary, there will be a strong likelihood that the myth of inferiority will be perpetuated in young people growing to maturity, and for youngsters coming into the world for decades hence. It will be as if they were told, "Here in our Dene nation, we do our own thing. We are cut off to some extent from the evils of 'white' society. We consider ourselves Canadians, but with a difference. We are aborigines, and because we are

Indians and afraid to take our place among other Canadians, we regretfully conclude we are inferior."

Mr. Justice Berger, in a speech to the Southern Alberta Institute of Technology, has said the Mackenzie pipeline will be "across a land where four different races live, speaking seven different languages..."

Men of the North, let us prove to Mr. Berger, and to all other Canadians, that the pipeline will be built across a land where men, women and children, each one different from the other, live together in harmony, where there is respect for all and ill will toward none.

Let us all, as Canadians, march together to a Northern dawn, as bright and promising as the excitement and splendor of a sunrise on our Mackenzie River.

The following is a facsimile of Treaty 11 and the pertinent parts of Treaty 8 that leave no doubt that the participating tribes clearly understood that "...said Indians do hereby cede, release, surrender and yield up to the Government of the Dominion of Canada, for His Majesty the King and His Successors forever, all their rights, titles and privileges whatsoever to the lands included within the following limits..."

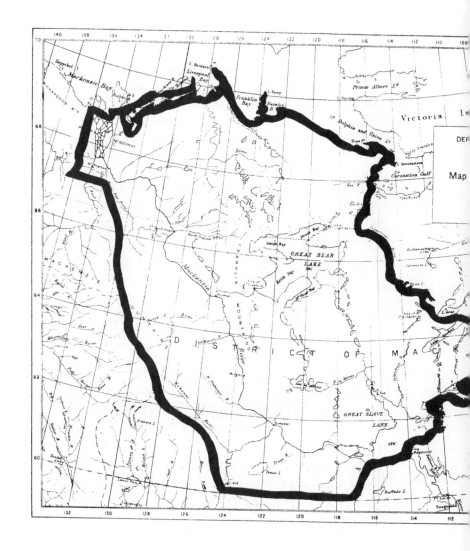

TREATY No. 11

(JUNE 27, 1921)

AND

ADHESION

(JULY 17, 1922)

WITH REPORTS, ETC.

Reprinted from the edition of 1926 by

EDMOND CLOUTIER, C.M.G., O.A., D.S.P.
QUEEN'S PRINTER AND CONTROLLER OF STATIONERY
OTTAWA, 1957

90199—1

REPORT OF THE
COMMISSIONER FOR TREATY No. 11

OTTAWA, October 12, 1921.

D. C. SCOTT, Esq.,
   Deputy Superintendent General,
      Department of Indian Affairs,
         Ottawa.

SIR,—I have the honour to submit herewith the report on treaty made by me on authority granted by Order in Council, dated March 14, last, as Commissioner to negotiate a treaty with the Indians occupying the territory north of the 60th parallel and along the Mackenzie river and the Arctic ocean.

I left Edmonton on June 8, 1921, accompanied by Inspector W. B. Bruce, Constable Wood and Constable Campbell, of the Royal Canadian Mounted Police. Constable Campbell acted as my clerk for the summer.

Arriving at Fort McMurray on June 11, we left there on the 14th in a houseboat, the property of the Hudson's Bay Company, which company had made all arrangements for the transportation of the treaty party during the summer in the North.

We arrived at Fort Fitzgerald on June 18, crossed the portage to Fort Smith, and boarded the ss. *Mackenzie River* on June 20 for Fort Providence, at which place the first adhesion to Treaty 11 was to be taken. July 5 was the date set for the meeting of the Indians and myself to take place at Fort Providence, and, in order to arrive in good time, I thought it better for me and my party to proceed there by the ss. *Mackenzie River*, and let the houseboat take us up again at this point. The transportation of the houseboat across the portage at Fort Smith took several days.

On our arrival at Fort Providence, on June 20, I found the Indians were not at the post, as we were there before the date set for the meeting, so word was sent of my arrival, and the majority of the Providence Indians living at Willow Lake arrived on June 25, those at Trout Lake not till July 2. I had several meetings with them, and explained the terms of treaty. They were very apt in asking questions, and here, as in all the other posts where the treaty was signed, the questions asked and the difficulties encountered were much the same. The Indians seemed afraid, for one thing, that their liberty to hunt, trap and fish would be taken away or curtailed, but were assured by me that this would not be the case, and the Government will expect them to support themselves in their own way, and, in fact, that more twine for nets and more ammunition were given under the terms of this treaty than under any of the preceding ones; this went a long way to calm their fears. I also pointed out that any game laws made were to their advantage, and, whether they took treaty or not, they were subject to the laws of the Dominion. They also seemed afraid that they would be liable for military service if the treaty was signed, that they would be confined on the reserves, but, when told that they were exempt from military service, and that the reserves mentioned in the treaty would be of their own choosing, for their own use, and not for the white people, and that they would be free to come and go as they pleased, they were satisfied.

3

Practically all the bands dealt with wanted more provision for medical attendance at each post, schools for their children, and supplies for their old and destitute. I pointed out that they were still able to make their own living, and that Dr. A. L. McDonald, of the Indian Department, was then with me, and that they could see him, and that he would attend them free if they wished, but that it was impossible for the Government to furnish regular medical attention, when they were occupying such a vast tract of territory. Schools were already established, and their children receiving free education, and supplies were left at each point for the sick and destitute.

The treaty was signed at Fort Providence on June 27, and the following were paid:—

    1 Chief,
    2 Headmen, and
    255 others.

Our houseboat arrived on July 5, and we left Providence for Fort Simpson on the 7th, securing adhesion to the treaty there on July 11.

    1 Chief,
    2 Headmen, and
    344 other Indians were paid.

Adhesions to the treaty were obtained at Fort Wrigley on July 13.

    1 Headman, and
    77 others were paid.

At Fort Norman on July 15,—

    1 Chief,
    2 Headmen, and
    205 others were paid.

At Good Hope, July 21,—

    1 Chief,
    1 Headman, and
    208 others were paid.

At Arctic Red River on July 26,—

    1 Chief,
    1 Headman, and
    169 others were paid.

At Fort McPherson on July 28,—

    1. Chief,
    1 Headman, and
    217 others were paid.

At Fort Rae on August 22,—

    1 Chief,
    2 Headmen, and
    440 others were paid.

Practically all the Indians were dealt with at Fort Providence, Simpson, Wrigley, Arctic Red River and McPherson, and about 65 per cent at Fort Norman, Fort Good Hope and Rae, the remainder of these Indians having been at these posts in the spring and left word that they were willing to take treaty, but had to return to their hunting grounds for their summer's work.

At Fort Rae is the largest band of Indians, about 800, and this is the most inaccessible, being on the arm of Great Slave lake, difficulty in crossing this lake being experienced, more especially in the late summer and fall on account of storms, our party being stormbound at Hay River for five days prior to crossing. These Indians hunt in every direction from the fort, some as far as 200 miles, and only come to the post in spring to trade their furs, so that, in future, I would suggest that this be the first post visited when making payments.

We crossed the lake from Hay River to Rae in the Hudson Bay schooner *Fort Rae*, leaving our houseboat to take us up at Resolution, from which place we went on August 25, arriving at Fort Smith on August 30, Fort McMurray and Edmonton in September.

I much regret that I was unable, owing to the lack of time, to visit Fort Liard, and secure adhesion to the treaty by the Indians at that point, although they had sent word to Fort Simpson of their willingness to accept the same. I considered it advisable to proceed to Great Slave Lake, and cross to Fort Rae at the first opportunity, as the season was getting late.

Dr. A. L. McDonald joined the party at Fort Providence, and accompanied it to Good Hope, at that place having to return to Fort Resolution on account of smallpox having been reported, which report, fortunately, proved untrue. He joined the party again at Hay River, and remained with it until arrival at his headquarters at Fort Smith.

I was very glad to be accompanied by His Lordship Bishop Breynat, O.M.I., who has considerable influence with the Indians in the North, and would like here to express my appreciation of the help and hospitality accorded to me and my party in his missions, and I desire also to express my appreciation of the services rendered by Inspector Bruce, of the Royal Canadian Mounted Police, and by his party. Constables Woods and Campbell performed their duties in the most creditable manner.

The actual number of Indians paid was:—

7 Chiefs at $32 each	} .... $	488
12 Headmen at $22 each		

and

1,915 Indians at $12 each....................... $22,980

H. A. CONROY,
Commissioner, Treaty No. 11.

TREATY NUMBER ELEVEN

ARTICLES OF A TREATY made and concluded on the several dates mentioned therein in the year of Our Lord One thousand Nine hundred and Twenty-One, between His Most Gracious Majesty George V, King of Great Britain and Ireland and of the British Dominions beyond the Seas, by His Commissioner, Henry Anthony Conroy, Esquire, of the City of Ottawa, of the One Part, and the Slave, Dogrib, Loucheux, Hare and other Indians, inhabitants of the territory within the limits hereinafter defined and described, by their Chiefs and Headmen, hereunto subscribed, of the other part:—

WHEREAS, the Indians inhabiting the territory hereinafter defined have been convened to meet a commissioner representing His Majesty's Government of the Dominion of Canada at certain places in the said territory in this present year of 1921, to deliberate upon certain matters of interest to His Most Gracious Majesty, of the one part, and the said Indians of the other.

AND WHEREAS, the said Indians have been notified and informed by His Majesty's said commissioner that it is His desire to open for settlement, immigration, trade, travel, mining, lumbering and such other purposes as to His

158

Majesty may seem meet, a tract of country bounded and described as hereinafter set forth, and to obtain the consent thereto of His Indian subjects inhabiting the said tract, and to make a treaty, so that there may be peace and goodwill between them and His Majesty's other subjects, and that His Indian people may know and be assured of what allowances they are to expect and receive from His Majesty's bounty and benevolence.

AND WHEREAS, the Indians of the said tract, duly convened in council at the respective points named hereunder, and being requested by His Majesty's Commissioner, to name certain Chiefs and Headmen, who should be authorized on their behalf to conduct such negotiations and sign any treaty to be founded thereon, and to become responsible to His Majesty for the faithful performance by their respective bands of such obligations as shall be assumed by them, the said Indians have therefore acknowledged for that purpose the several chiefs and Headmen who have subscribed thereto.

AND WHEREAS the said Commissioner has proceeded to negotiate a treaty with the Slave, Dogrib, Loucheux, Hare and other Indians inhabiting the district hereinafter defined and described, which has been agreed upon and concluded by the respective bands at the dates mentioned hereunder, the said Indians do hereby cede, release, surrender and yield up to the Government of the Dominion of Canada, for His Majesty the King and His Successors forever, all their rights, titles, and privileges whatsoever to the lands included within the following limits, that is to say:

Commencing at the northwesterly corner of the territory ceded under the provisions of Treaty Number Eight; thence northeasterly along the height-of-land to the point where it intersects the boundary between the Yukon Territory and the Northwest Territories; thence northwesterly along the said boundary to the shore of the Arctic ocean; thence easterly along the said shore to the mouth of the Coppermine river; thence southerly and southeasterly along the left bank of the said river to Lake Gras by way of Point lake; thence along the southern shore of Lake Gras to a point situated northwest of the most western extremity of Aylmer lake; thence along the southern shore of Aylmer lake and following the right bank of the Lockhart river to Artillery lake; thence along the western shore of Artillery lake and following the right bank of the Lockhart river to the site of Old Fort Reliance where the said river enters Great Slave lake, this being the northeastern corner of the territory ceded under the provisions of Treaty Number Eight; thence westerly along the northern boundary of the said territory so ceded to the point of commencement; comprising an area of approximately three hundred and seventy-two thousand square miles.

AND ALSO, the said Indian rights, titles and privileges whatsoever to all other lands wherever situated in the Yukon Territory, the Northwest Territories or in any other portion of the Dominion of Canada.

To have and to hold the same to His Majesty the King and His Successors forever.

AND His Majesty the King hereby agrees with the said Indians that they shall have the right to pursue their usual vocations of hunting, trapping and fishing throughout the tract surrendered as heretofore described, subject to such regulations as may from time to time be made by the Government of the Country acting under the authority of His Majesty, and saving and excepting such tracts as may be required or taken up from time to time for settlement, mining, lumbering, trading or other purposes.

AND His Majesty the King hereby agrees and undertakes to lay aside reserves for each band, the same not to exceed in all one square mile for each family of five, or in that proportion for larger or smaller families;

PROVIDED, however, that His Majesty reserves the right to deal with any settlers within the boundaries of any lands reserved for any band as He may see fit; and also that the aforesaid reserves of land, or any interest therein, may be sold or otherwise disposed of by His Majesty's Government for the use and benefit of the said Indians entitled thereto, with their consent first had and obtained; but in no wise shall the said Indians, or any of them, be entitled to sell or otherwise alienate any of the lands allotted to them as reserves.

It is further agreed between His Majesty and His Indian subjects that such portions of the reserves and lands above indicated as may at any time be required for public works, buildings, railways, or roads of whatsoever nature may be appropriated for that purpose by His Majesty's Government of the Dominion of Canada, due compensation being made to the Indians for the value of any improvements thereon, and an equivalent in land, money or other consideration for the area of the reserve so appropriated.

And in order to show the satisfaction of His Majesty with the behaviour and good conduct of His Indian subjects, and in extinguishment of all their past claims hereinabove mentioned, He hereby, through his Commissioner, agrees to give to each Chief a present of thirty-two dollars in cash, to each Headman, twenty-two dollars, and to every other Indian of whatever age of the families represented, at the time and place of payment, twelve dollars.

HIS MAJESTY, also agrees that during the coming year, and annually thereafter, He will cause to be paid to the said Indians in cash, at suitable places and dates, of which the said Indians shall be duly notified, to each Chief twenty-five dollars, to each Headman fifteen dollars, and to every other Indian of whatever age five dollars, to be paid only to heads of families for the members thereof, it being provided for the purposes of this Treaty that each band having at least thirty members may have a Chief, and that in addition to a Chief, each band may have Councillors or Headmen in the proportion of two to each two hundred members of the band.

FURTHER, His Majesty agrees that each Chief shall receive once and for all a silver medal, a suitable flag and a copy of this Treaty for the use of his band; and during the coming year, and every third year thereafter, each Chief and Headman shall receive a suitable suit of clothing.

FURTHER, His Majesty agrees to pay the salaries of teachers to instruct the children of said Indians in such manner as His Majesty's Government may deem advisable.

FURTHER, His Majesty agrees to supply once and for all to each Chief of a band that selects a reserve, ten axes, five hand-saws, five augers, one grindstone, and the necessary files and whetstones for the use of the band.

FURTHER, His Majesty agrees that, each band shall receive once and for all equipment for hunting, fishing and trapping to the value of fifty dollars for each family of such band, and that there shall be distributed annually among the Indians equipment, such as twine for nets, ammunition and trapping to the value of three dollars per head for each Indian who continues to follow the vocation of hunting, fishing and trapping.

FURTHER, His Majesty agrees that, in the event of any of the Indians aforesaid being desirous of following agricultural pursuits, such Indians shall receive such assistance as is deemed necessary for that purpose.

AND the undersigned Slave, Dogrib, Loucheux, Hare and other Chiefs and Headmen, on their own behalf and on behalf of all the Indians whom they represent, do hereby solemnly promise and engage to strictly observe this Treaty, and also to conduct and behave themselves as good loyal subjects of His Majesty the King.

THEY promise and engage that they will, in all respects, obey and abide by the law; that they will maintain peace between themselves and others of His Majesty's subjects, whether Indians, half-breeds or whites, now inhabiting and hereafter to inhabit any part of the said ceded territory; that they will not molest the person or property of any inhabitant of such ceded tract, or of any other district or country, or interfere with, or trouble any person passing or travelling through the said tract or any part thereof, and that they will assist the officers of His Majesty in bringing to justice and punishment any Indian offending against the stipulations of this Treaty, or infringing the law in force in the country so ceded.

IN WITNESS WHEREOF, His Majesty's said Commissioner and the said Chiefs and Headmen have hereunto set their hands at the places and times set forth in the year herein first above written.

SIGNED AT PROVIDENCE on the twenty-seventh day of June, 1921, by His Majesty's Commissioner and the Chiefs and Headmen in the presence of the undersigned witnesses, after having been first interpreted and explained.

WITNESSES:

W. V. BRUCE, *Insp. R.C.M.P.*,	H. A. CONROY, *Comm.*
F. H. KITTO,	PAUL LAFOIN x *Chief,* his mark
A. H. MILLER,	HARRY FRANCIS x *Headman,* his mark
G. BREYNAT, O.M.I., *Bishop of Adr.,* *Vic. Apost. of Mackenzie,*	
J. A. R. BALSILLIE.	BAPTISTE SABOURINE x *Headman.* his mark

SIGNED at Simpson on the eleventh day of July, 1921, by His Majesty's Commissioner and the Chiefs and Headmen in the presence of the undersigned witnesses, after having been first interpreted and explained.

WITNESSES:
(Sgd.)

G. BREYNAT, O.M.I., *Bishop of Adr.,* *Vic. Apost. of Mackenzie,* JOHN G. CORRY, W. V. BRUCE, *Insp. R.C.M.P.*, A. F. CAMSELL, T. W. HARRIS.	H. A. CONROY, *Comm.* (ANTOINE) ᐊᒍᐅ (KORWERGEN) ᑕ ᑭᐊᓇ᙮ BEDSEDIA x his mark

SIGNED at Wrigley on the thirteenth day of July, 1921, by His Majesty's Commissioner and the Chiefs and Headmen in the presence of the undersigned witnesses, after having been first interpreted and explained.

WITNESSES:
(Sgd.)

G. BREYNAT, O.M.I., *Bishop of Adr.,* *Vic. Apost. of Mackenzie,* W. V. BRUCE, *Insp. R.C.M.P.*, A. L. McDONALD, F. H. BACON.	H. A. CONROY, *Comm.* (YENDO) ᑕᐅ

SIGNED at Norman on the fifteenth day of July, 1921, by His Majesty's Commissioner and the Chiefs and Headmen in the presence of the undersigned witnesses, after having been first interpreted and explained.

WITNESSES:
(Sgd.)
G. BREYNAT, O.M.I., *Bishop of Adr.,*
   Vic. Apost. of Mackenzie,
W. V. BRUCE, *Insp. R.C.M.P.,*
GEO. P. JOHNSTON,
G. H. M. CAMPBELL, *Const. R.C.M.P.*

H. A. CONROY, *Comm.*

ALBERT WRIGHT,

SAUL BLONDIN x
     his
     mark

SIGNED at Good Hope on the twenty-first day of July, 1921, by His Majesty's Commissioner and the Chiefs and Headmen in the presence of the undersigned witnesses, after having been first interpreted and explained.

WITNESSES:
(Sgd.)
G. BREYNAT, O.M.I., *Bishop of Adr.,*
   Vic. Apost. of Mackenzie
W. V. BRUCE, *Insp. R.C.M.P.*
F. H. BACON,
J. H. BRASHAR, *Cpl. R.C.M.P.*

H. A. CONROY, *Comm.*

SIMEON x
    his
    mark

FRANCOIS x NATEGAL.
    his
    mark

SIGNED at Arctic Red River on the twenty-sixth day of July, 1921, by His Majesty's Commissioner and the Chiefs and Headmen in the presence of the undersigned witnesses, after having been first interpreted and explained.

WITNESSES:
(Sgd.)
G. BREYNAT, O.M.I., *Bishop of Adr.,*
   Vic. Apost. of Mackenzie,
W. V. BRUCE, *Insp. R.C.M.P.,*
J. LECUYER, Pr. O.M.I.
J. PARSONS.

H. A. CONROY, *Comm.*

PAUL x
    his
    mark

NIDE APHI,
FABIEN-LALOO.

SIGNED at McPherson on the twenty-eighth day of July, 1921, by His Majesty's Commissioner and the Chiefs and Headmen in the presence of the undersigned witnesses, after having been first interpreted and explained.

WITNESSES:
(Sgd.)
W. V. BRUCE, *Insp. R.C.M.P.,*
J. PARSONS,
F. H. BACON.
JAMES FIRTH.

H. A. CONROY, *Comm.*

JABY LALO,

JOHNNIE KIKAWCHIK.

SIGNED at Liard on the   day of   , 1921, by His Majesty's Commissioner and the Chiefs and Headmen in the presence of the undersigned witnesses, after having been first interpreted and explained.

WITNESSES:

SIGNED at Rae on the twenty-second day of August, 1921, by His Majesty's Commissioner and the Chiefs and Headmen in the presence of the undersigned witnesses, after having been first interpreted and explained.

WITNESSES:
(Sgd.)
G. BREYNAT, O.M.I., *Bishop of Adr.,*
    Vic. Apost. of Mackenzie,
W. J. O'DONNELL,
W. V. BRUCE, *Insp. R.C.M.P.,*
ED. HERON, H. B. Co.
CLAUDE WM. LAFOUNTAIN,

H. A. CONROY, *Comm.,*
        his
MORPHY x
        mark
        his
JERMAIN x
        mark
        his
JOSUE x BEAULIEU.
        mark

ORDER IN COUNCIL

RATIFYING TREATY No. 11

P.C. 3985

PRIVY COUNCIL CANADA

AT THE GOVERNMENT HOUSE AT OTTAWA,

SATURDAY, the 22nd day of October, 1921.

PRESENT:

HIS EXCELLENCY THE GOVERNOR GENERAL IN COUNCIL

WHEREAS the Superintendent General of Indian Affairs submits herewith Treaty Number Eleven made, in accordance with the terms of Order in Council of 14th March, 1921 (P.C. 686), by Henry Anthony Conroy, Esquire, who was appointed a Commissioner by the said Order in Council, to negotiate with the Slave, Dogrib, Loucheux, Hare and other Indians for the cession, by the said Indians to the Crown of all their rights, titles and privileges whatsoever in the territory north of the sixtieth parallel and along the Mackenzie river and the Arctic ocean in the Dominion of Canada.

THEREFORE His Excellency the Governor General in Council, on the recommendation of the Superintendent General of Indian Affairs, is pleased to ratify the said Treaty Number Eleven, made and negotiated as hereinbefore recited, and the same is hereby ratified and confirmed accordingly.

RODOLPHE BOUDREAU,
Clerk of the Privy Council.

The Honourable

The Superintendent General of Indian Affairs.

Owing to the death of Commissioner Conroy on April 27, 1922, and to the fact that he had not had an opportunity during the summer of 1921 of obtaining the adhesion to the Treaty by the Slave Indians of the Liard district, it was necessary to make other arrangements. Accordingly the authority of His Excellency the Governor General in Council was obtained for the appointment of T. W. Harris, Indian agent at Fort Simpson, N.W.T., as Commissioner to secure this adhesion.

163

Following is a copy of the Order in Council:—

P.C. 993

CERTIFIED COPY *of a Report of the Committee of the Privy Council approved by His Excellency the Governor General on the 9th May, 1922*

The Committee of the Privy Council have had before them a Report, dated 2nd May, 1922, from the Superintendent General of Indian Affairs, submitting,— with reference to Order in Council of the 14th March, 1921, under which Mr. H. A. Conroy, Inspector for Treaty No. 8, was authorized to act as Commissioner to negotiate a Treaty (known as Treaty No. 11) with the Indians occupying the territory north of the 60th parallel and along the Mackenzie river to the Arctic coast,—that owing to lack of time Mr. Conroy was unable to visit the Fort Liard Indians last year with a view to securing their adhesion to the treaty.

The Minister states that owing to Mr. Conroy's death, which occurred on the 27th April, 1922, it is essential that someone should be deputed to complete the treaty negotiations.

The Minister, therefore, recommends that Mr. T. W. Harris, Indian agent at Fort Simpson, N.W.T., be authorized to complete the work entrusted to the late Mr. Conroy in connection with the treaty above mentioned.

The Committee concur in the foregoing recommendation and submit the same for approval.

RODOLPHE BOUDREAU,
Clerk of the Privy Council.

The Honourable

The Superintendent General of Indian Affairs.

Accordingly Commissioner Harris, accompanied by His Lordship Bishop Breynat and Reverend Father Moisan, visited Fort Liard on July 17th. The terms of the treaty having been explained by the Commissioner, the Chief and Headmen, who had previously been elected, signed the treaty on behalf of the Indians as indicated in the following Indenture:—

SIGNED at Liard on the seventeenth day of July, 1922, by His Majesty's Commissioner and the Chiefs and Headmen in the presence of the undersigned witnesses, after having been first interpreted and explained.

WITNESSES:

(Sgd.)

(Sgd.)

THOMAS WILLIAM HARRIS, *Comm.*

G. BREYNAT, O.M.I., *Bishop of Adr.,*
Vic. Ap. of Mackenzie

THOMAS E. KINLA x *Chief,*
his / mark

F. MOISAN, O.M.I. *Ptre.*
A. BORBIN, *Const. R.C.M.P.,*
JOSEPH BERRAULT, *Interpreter.*

JOSEPH FANTASQUR x *Headman,*
his / mark

DAVID CELIBETA x *Headman.*
his / mark

The Number of Indians paid was:—

1 Chief at $32	$	32
2 Headmen at $22		44
147 Indians at $12		1,764

164

ORDER IN COUNCIL

RATIFYING ADHESION TO TREATY No. 11

March 29, 1923.

The Committee of the Privy Council, on the recommendation of the Superintendent General of Indian Affairs, submit herewith for ratification and confirmation by Your Excellency in Council, an instrument, in duplicate, containing the adhesion to Treaty No. 11 of the Indians of Fort Liard taken the seventeenth day of July, 1922, by Mr. T. W. Harris, who was appointed by an. Order of Your Excellency in Council of 9th May, 1922 (P.C. No. 993), as His Majesty's Commissioner to take the said adhesion; one copy of the instrument to be returned to the Department of Indian Affairs and the other to be kept on record in the Privy Council Office.

(Sgd.)　　RODOLPHE BOUDREAU,
Clerk of the Privy Council.

The Honourable
　　The Superintendent General of Indian Affairs.

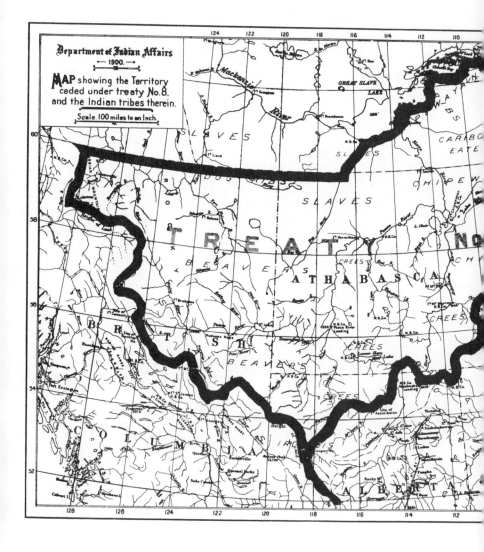

Department of Indian Affairs
— 1900. —

MAP showing the Territory ceded under treaty No.8. and the Indian tribes therein.

Scale. 100 miles to an Inch.

TREATY No. 8

MADE JUNE 21, 1899

AND

ADHESIONS, REPORTS, ETC.

(only part of Treaty
Eight is reprinted here)

STATEMENT of Indians paid Annuity and Gratuity, &c.—*Concluded.*

—	Chiefs.	Head-men.	Other Indians.	Cash Paid each Band.	Total Cash Paid.
				$ cts.	$ cts.
FORT McMURRAY.					
Cree and Chipewyan Bands—					
Headmen......	....	2	....	44 00	
Other Indians......	....	....	130	1,560 00	
					1,604 00
WABISCOW.					
Cree Band—					
Chief......	1	....	....	32 00	
Headmen......	....	4	....	88 00	
Other Indians......	....	....	191	2,292 00	
					2,412 00
Total......	7	23	2,187	....	26,974 00

SUMMARY.

7 Chiefs at $32......	$	224 00
23 Headmen at $22......		506 00
2,187 Other Indians at $12......		26,224 00
2,217......	$	26,974 00

Certified correct,

DAVID LAIRD,
J. H. ROSS,
J. A. J. McKENNA.
Indian Treaty Commissioners.

WINNIPEG, MAN., September 22, 1899.

TREATY No. 8.

ARTICLES OF A TREATY made and concluded at the several dates mentioned therein, in the year of Our Lord one thousand eight hundred and ninety-nine, between Her most Gracious Majesty the Queen of Great Britain and Ireland, by Her Commissioners the Honourable David Laird, of Winnipeg, Manitoba, Indian Commissioner for the said Province and the Northwest Territories; James Andrew Joseph McKenna, of Ottawa, Ontario, Esquire, and the Honourable James Hamilton Ross, of Regina, in the Northwest Territories, of the one part; and the Cree, Beaver, Chipewyan and other Indians, inhabitants of the territory within the limits hereinafter defined and described, by their Chiefs and Headmen, hereunto subscribed, of the other part:—

WHEREAS, the Indians inhabiting the territory hereinafter defined have, pursuant to notice given by the Honourable Superintendant General of Indian Affairs in the year 1898, been convened to meet a Commission representing Her Majesty's Government of the Dominion of Canada at certain places in the said territory in this present year 1899, to deliberate upon certain matters of interest to Her Most Gracious Majesty, of the one part, and the said Indians of the other.

AND WHEREAS, the said Indians have been notified and informed by Her Majesty's said Commission that it is Her desire to open for settlement, immigration, trade, travel, mining, lumbering, and such other purposes as to Her

Majesty may seem meet, a tract of country bounded and described as hereinafter mentioned, and to obtain the consent thereto of Her Indian subjects inhabiting the said tract, and to make a treaty, and arrange with them, so that there may be peace and good will between them and Her Majesty's other subjects, and that Her Indian people may know and be assured of what allowances they are to count upon and receive from Her Majesty's bounty and benevolence.

AND WHEREAS, the Indians of the said tract, duly convened in council at the respective points named hereunder, and being requested by Her Majesty's Commissioners to name certain Chiefs and Headmen who should be authorized on their behalf to conduct such negotiations and sign any treaty to be founded thereon, and to become responsible to Her Majesty for the faithful performance by their respective bands of such obligations as shall be assumed by them, the said Indians have therefore acknowledged for that purpose the several Chiefs and Headmen who have subscribed hereto.

AND WHEREAS, the said Commissioners have proceeded to negotiate a treaty with the Cree, Beaver, Chipewyan and other Indians, inhabiting the district hereinafter defined and described, and the same has been agreed upon and concluded by the respective bands at the dates mentioned hereunder, the said Indians DO HEREBY CEDE, RELEASE, SURRENDER AND YIELD UP to the Government of the Dominion of Canada, for Her Majesty the Queen and Her successors for ever, all their rights, titles and privileges whatsoever, to the lands included within the following limits, that is to say:—

Commencing at the source of the main branch of the Red Deer River in Alberta, thence due west to the central range of the Rocky Mountains, thence northwesterly along the said range to the point where it intersects the 60th parallel of north latitude, thence east along said parallel to the point where it intersects Hay River, thence northeasterly down said river to the south shore of Great Slave Lake, thence along the said shore northeasterly (and including such rights to the islands in said lakes as the Indians mentioned in the treaty may possess), and thence easterly and northeasterly along the south shores of Christie's Bay and McLeod's Bay to old Fort Reliance near the mouth of Lockhart's River, thence southeasterly in a straight line to and including Black Lake, thence southwesterly up the stream from Cree Lake, thence including said lake southwesterly along the height of land between the Athabasca and Churchill Rivers to where it intersects the northern boundary of Treaty Six, and along the said boundary easterly, northerly and southwesterly, to the place of commencement.

AND ALSO the said Indian rights, titles and privileges whatsoever to all other lands wherever situated in the Northwest Territories, British Columbia, or in any other portion of the Dominion of Canada.

To HAVE AND TO HOLD the same to Her Majesty the Queen and Her successors for ever.

And Her Majesty the Queen HEREBY AGREES with the said Indians that they shall have right to pursue their usual vocations of hunting, trapping and fishing throughout the tract surrendered as heretofore described, subject to such regulations as may from time to time be made by the Government of the country, acting under the authority of Her Majesty, and saving and excepting such tracts as may be required or taken up from time to time for settlement, mining, lumbering, trading or other purposes.

And Her Majesty the Queen hereby agrees and undertakes to lay aside reserves for such bands as desire reserves, the same not to exceed in all one square mile for each family of five for such number of families as may elect to reside on reserves, or in that proportion for larger or smaller families; and for such families or individual Indians as may prefer to live apart from band reserves,

Her Majesty undertakes to provide land in severalty to the extent of 160 acres to each Indian, the land to be conveyed with a proviso as to non-alienation without the consent of the Governor General in Council of Canada, the selection of such reserves, and lands in severalty, to be made in the manner following, namely, the Superintendent General of Indian Affairs shall depute and send a suitable person to determine and set apart such reserves and lands, after consulting with the Indians concerned as to the locality which may be found suitable and open for selection.

Provided, however, that Her Majesty reserves the right to deal with any settlers within the bounds of any lands reserved for any band as She may see fit; and also that the aforesaid reserves of land, or any interest therein, may be sold or otherwise disposed of by Her Majesty's Government for the use and benefit of the said Indians entitled thereto, with their consent first had and obtained.

It is further agreed between Her Majesty and Her said Indian subjects that such portions of the reserves and lands above indicated as may at any time be required for public works, buildings, railways, or roads of whatsoever nature may be appropriated for that purpose by Her Majesty's Government of the Dominion of Canada, due compensation being made to the Indians for the value of any improvements thereon, and an equivalent in land, money or other consideration for the area of the reserve so appropriated.

And with a view to show the satisfaction of Her Majesty with the behaviour and good conduct of Her Indians, and in extinguishment of all their past claims, She hereby, through Her Commissioners, agrees to make each Chief a present of thirty-two dollars in cash, to each Headman twenty-two dollars, and to every other Indian of whatever age, of the families represented at the time and place of payment, twelve dollars.

Her Majesty also agrees that next year, and annually afterwards for ever, She will cause to be paid to the said Indians in cash, at suitable places and dates, of which the said Indians shall be duly notified, to each Chief twenty-five dollars, each Headman, not to exceed four to a large Band and two to a small Band, fifteen dollars, and to every other Indian, of whatever age, five dollars, the same, unless there be some exceptional reason, to be paid only to heads of families for those belonging thereto.

FURTHER, Her Majesty agrees that each Chief, after signing the treaty, shall receive a silver medal and a suitable flag, and next year, and every third year thereafter, each Chief and Headman shall receive a suitable suit of clothing.

FURTHER, Her Majesty agrees to pay the salaries of such teachers to instruct the children of said Indians as to Her Majesty's Government of Canada may seem advisable.

FURTHER, Her Majesty agrees to supply each Chief of a Band that selects a reserve, for the use of that Band, ten axes, five hand-saws, five augers, one grindstone, and the necessary files and whetstones.

FURTHER, Her Majesty agrees that each Band that elects to take a reserve and cultivate the soil, shall, as soon as convenient after such reserve is set aside and settled upon, and the Band has signified its choice and is prepared to break up the soil, receive two hoes, one spade, one scythe and two hay forks for every family so settled, and for every three families one plough and one harrow, and to the Chief, for the use of his Band, two horses or a yoke of oxen, and for each Band potatoes, barley, oats and wheat (if such seed be suited to the locality of the reserve), to plant the land actually broken up, and provisions for one month in the spring for several years while planting such seeds; and to every family one cow, and every Chief one bull, and one mowing-machine and one reaper for the use of his Band when it is ready for them; for such families as prefer to raise stock instead of cultivating the soil, every family of five persons, two cows, and every Chief two bulls and two mowing-machines when ready for their use, and a like proportion for smaller or larger families. The aforesaid articles, machines and cattle to be given one for all for the encouragement of agriculture and stock raising; and for such Bands as prefer to continue hunting and fishing, as much ammunition and twine for making nets annually as will amount in value to one dollar per head of the families so engaged in hunting and fishing.

And the undersigned Cree, Beaver, Chipewyan and other Indian Chiefs and Headmen, on their own behalf and on behalf of all the Indians whom they represent, DO HEREBY SOLEMNLY PROMISE and engage to strictly observe this Treaty, and also to conduct and behave themselves as good and loyal subjects of Her Majesty the Queen.

THEY PROMISE AND ENGAGE that they will, in all respects, obey and abide by the law; that they will maintain peace between each other, and between themselves and other tribes of Indians, and between themselves and others of Her Majesty's subjects, whether Indians, half-breeds or whites, this year inhabiting and hereafter to inhabit any part of the said ceded territory; and that they will not molest the person or property of any inhabitant of such ceded tract, or of any other district or country, or interfere with or trouble any person passing or travelling through the said tract or any part thereof, and that they will assist the officers of Her Majesty in bringing to justice and punishment any Indian offending against the stipulations of this Treaty or infringing the law in force in the country so ceded.

IN WITNESS WHEREOF Her Majesty's said Commissioners and the Cree Chief and Headmen of Lesser Slave Lake and the adjacent territory, HAVE HEREUNTO SET THEIR HANDS at Lesser Slave Lake on the twenty-first day of June, in the year herein first above written.

Signed by the parties hereto, in the presence of the undersigned witnesses, the same having been first explained to the Indians by Albert Tate and Samuel Cunningham, Interpreters.

Father A. LACOMBE,
GEO. HOLMES,
†E. GROUARD, O.M.I.
W. G. WHITE,
JAMES WALKER,
J. ARTHUR COTÉ,
A. E. SNYDER, Insp. N.W.M.P.,
H. B. ROUND,
HARRISON S. YOUNG,
J. F. PRUD'HOMME,
J. W. MARTIN,
C. MAIR,
H. A. CONROY,
PIERRE DESCHAMBEAULT,
J. H. PICARD,
RICHARD SECORD,
M. McCAULEY.

DAVID LAIRD, *Treaty Commissioner,*
J. A. J. McKENNA, *Treaty Commissioner,*
J. H. ROSS, *Treaty Commissioner,*
                    his
KEE NOO SHAY OO x *Chief,*
                    mark
                    his
MOOSTOOS x *Headman,*
            mark
                    his
FELIX GIROUX x *Headman,*
            mark
                    his
WEE CHEE WAY SIS x *Headman,*
            mark
                    his
CHARLES NEE SUE TA SIS x *Headman,*
                    mark
                    his
CAPTAIN x *Headman,* from Sturgeon
            mark   Lake.

In witness whereof the Chairman of Her Majesty's Commissioners and the Headman of the Indians of Peace River Landing and the adjacent territory, in behalf of himself and the Indians whom he represents, have hereunto set their hands at the said Peace River Landing on the first day of July in the year of Our Lord one thousand eight hundred and ninety-nine.

Signed by the parties hereto, in the presence of the undersigned witnesses, the same having been first explained to the Indians by Father A. Lacombe and John Boucher, interpreters.

DAVID LAIRD, *Chairman of Indian Treaty Commissioners,*
his
DUNCAN x TASTAOOSTS, *Headman of*
mark *Crees*

A. LACOMBE.
†E. GROUARD, O.M.I., Ev. d'Ibora,
GEO. HOLMES,
HENRY McCORRISTER,
K. F. ANDERSON, Sgt., N.W.M.P.
PIERRE DESCHAMBEAULT,
H. A. CONROY,
T. A. BRICK,
HARRISON S. YOUNG,
J. W. MARTIN,
DAVID CURRY.

In witness whereof the Chairman of Her Majesty's Commissioners and the Chief and Headmen of the Beaver and Headman of the Crees and other Indians of Vermilion and the adjacent territory, in behalf of themselves and the Indians whom they represent, have hereunto set their hands at Vermilion on the eighth day of July, in the year of our Lord one thousand eight hundred and ninety-nine.

Signed by the parties hereto in the presence of the undersigned witnesses, the same having been first explained to the Indians by Father A. Lacombe and John Bourassa, Interpreters.

DAVID LAIRD,
Chairman of Indian Treaty Coms.,
his
AMBROSE x TETE NOIRE, *Chief Beaver*
mark *Indians.*
his
PIERROT x FOURNIER, *Headman Beaver*
mark *Indians.*
his *Headman*
KUIS KUIS KOW CA POOHOO x *Cree*
mark *Indians.*

A. LACOMBE,
†E. GROUARD, O.M.I., Ev. d'Ibora,
MALCOLM SCOTT,
F. D. WILSON, H. B. Co.,
H. A. CONROY,
PIERRE DESCHAMBEAULT,
HARRISON S. YOUNG,
J. W. MARTIN,
A. P. CLARKE,
CHAS. H. STUART WADE,
K. F. ANDERSON, Sgt., N.W.M.P.

In witness whereof the Chairman of Her Majesty's Treaty Commissioners and the Chief and Headman of the Chipewyan Indians of Fond du Lac (Lake Athabasca) and the adjacent territory, in behalf of themselves and the Indians whom they represent, have hereunto set their hands at the said Fond du Lac on the twenty-fifth and twenty-seventh days of July, in the year of Our Lord one thousand eight hundred and ninety-nine.

Signed by the parties hereto in the presence of the undersigned witnesses, the same having been first explained to the Indians by Pierre Deschambeault, Reverend Father Douceur and Louis Robillard, Interpreters.

DAVID LAIRD,
Chairman of Indian Treaty Coms.,
his
LAURENT x DZIEDDIN, *Headman*,
mark
his
TOUSSAINT x *Headman*,
mark

(The number accepting treaty being larger than at first expected, a Chief was allowed, who signed the treaty on the 27th July before the same witnesses to signatures of the Commissioner and Headman on the 25th.)

his
MAURICE x PICHE, *Chief of Band.*
mark
Witness, H. S. YOUNG.

G. BREYNAT, O.M.I.,
HARRISON S. YOUNG,
PIERRE DESCHAMBEAULT,
WILLIAM HENRY BURKE,
BATHURST F. COOPER,
GERMAIN MERCREDI,
his
LOUIS x ROBILLARD,
mark
K. F. ANDERSON, *Sgt., N.W.M.P.*

The Beaver Indians of Dunvegan having met on this sixth day of July, in this present year 1899, Her Majesty's. Commissioners, the Honourable James Hamilton Ross and James Andrew Joseph McKenna, Esquire, and having had explained to then the terms of the Treaty unto which the Chief and Headmen of the Indians of Lesser Slave Lake and adjacent country set their hands on the twenty-first day of June, in the year herein first above written, do join in the cession made by the said Treaty, and agree to adhere to the terms thereof in consideration of the undertakings made therein.

In witness whereof Her Majesty's said Commissioners and the Headman of the said Beaver Indians have hereunto set their hands at Dunvegan on this sixth day of July, in the year herein first above written.

Signed by the parties thereto in the presence of the undersigned witnesses, after the same had been read and explained to the Indians by the Reverend Joseph Le Treste and Peter Gunn, Interpreters.

J. H. ROSS,
J. A. J. McKENNA, } *Commissioners,*
his
NATOOSES x *Headman*,
mark

A. E. SNYDER, *Insp. N.W.M.P.*
J. LE TRESTE,
PETER GUNN,
F. J. FITZGERALD.

The Chipewyan Indians of Athabasca River, Birch River, Peace River, Slave River and Gull River, and the Cree Indians of Gull River and Deep Lake, having met at Fort Chipewyan on this thirteenth day of July, in this present year 1899, Her Majesty's Commissioners, the Honourable James Hamilton Ross and James Andrew Joseph McKenna, Esquire, and having had explained to them the terms of the Treaty unto which the Chief and Headmen of the Indians of Lesser Slave Lake and adjacent country set their hands on the twenty-first day of June, in the year herein first above written, do join in the cession made by the said Treaty, and agree to adhere to the terms thereof in consideration of the undertakings made therein.

In witness whereof Her Majesty's said Commissioners and the Chiefs and Headmen of the said Chipewyan and Cree Indians have hereunto set their hands at Fort Chipewyan on this thirteenth day of July, in the year herein first above written.

Signed by the parties thereto in the presence of the undersigned witnesses after the same had been read and explained to the Indians by Peter Mercredi, Chipewyan Interpreter, and George Drever, Cree Interpreter.

A. E. SNYDER, *Insp., N.W.M.P.*,
P. MERCREDI,
GEO. DREVER,
L. M. LE DOUSSAL,
A. DE CHAMBOUR, O.M.I.
H. B. ROUND,
GABRIEL BREYNAT, O.M.I.,
COLIN FRASER,
F. J. FITZGERALD,
B. F. COOPER,
H. W. McLAREN,

J. H. ROSS, *Treaty*
J. A. J. McKENNA, *Commissioners,*
his
ALEX. x LAVIOLETTE, *Chipewyan Chief,*
mark
his
JULIEN x RATFAT,
mark
his
SEPT. x HEEZELL, } *Chipewyan Headmen,*
mark
his
JUSTIN x MARTIN, *Cree Chief,*
mark
his
ANT. x TACCARROO, } *Cree Headmen.*
mark
his
THOMAS x GIBBOT,
mark

The Chipewyan Indians of Slave River and the country thereabouts having met at Smith's Landing on this seventeenth day of July, in this present year 1899, Her Majesty's Commissioners, the Honourable James Hamilton Ross and James Andrew Joseph McKenna, Esquire, and having had explained to them the terms of the Treaty unto which the Chief and Headmen of the Indians of Lesser Slave Lake and adjacent country, set their hands on the twenty-first day of June, in the year herein first above written, do join in the cession made by the said Treaty, and agree to adhere to the terms thereof in consideration of the undertakings made therein.

In witness whereof Her Majesty's said Commissioners and the Chief and Headmen of the said Chipewyan Indians have hereunto set their hands at Smith's Landing, on this seventeenth day of July, in the year herein first above written.

Signed by the parties thereto in the presence of the undersigned witnesses after the same had been read and explained to the Indians by John Trindle, Interpreter.

A. E. SNYDER, *Insp. N.W.M.P.*,
H. B. ROUND,
J. H. REID,
JAS. HALY,
JOHN TRINDLE,
F. J. FITZGERALD,
WM. McCLELLAND,
JOHN SUTHERLAND.

J. H. ROSS, *Treaty*
J. A. J. McKENNA, *Commissioners,*
his
PIERRE x SQUIRREL, *Chief,*
mark
his
MICHAEL x MAMDRILLE, *Headman,*
mark
his
WILLIAM x KISCORRAY, *Headman,*
mark

The Chipewyan and Cree Indians of Fort McMurray and the country there-abouts, having met at Fort McMurray, on this fourth day of August, in this present year 1899, Her Majesty's Commissioner, James Andrew Joseph McKenna, Esquire, and having had explained to them the terms of the Treaty unto which the Chief and Headmen of the Indians of Lesser Slave Lake and adjacent country set their hands on the twenty-first day of June, in the year herein first above written, do join in the cession made by the said Treaty and agree to adhere to the terms thereof in consideration of the undertakings made therein.

In witness whereof Her Majesty's said Commissioner and the Headmen of the said Chipewyan and Cree Indians have hereunto set their hands at Fort McMurray, on this fourth day of August, in the year herein first above written.

Signed by the parties thereto in the presence of the undersigned witnesses after the same had been read and explained to the Indians by the Rev. Father Lacombe and T. M. Clarke, Interpreters	J. A. J. McKenna, *Treaty Commis-* his *[sioner,* Adam x Boucher, *Chipewyan Head-* mark *[man,* his Seapotakinum x Cree, *Cree Headman,* mark

A. Lacombe, *O.M.I.*,
Arthur J. Warwick,
T. M. Clarke,
J. W. Martin,
F. J. Fitzgerald,
M. J. H. Vernon.

The Indians of Wapiscow and the country thereabouts having met at Wapiscow Lake on this fourteenth day of August, in this present year 1899, Her Majesty's Commissioner, the Honourable James Hamilton Ross, and having had explained to them the terms of the Treaty unto which the Chief and Head-men of the Indians of Lesser Slave Lake and adjacent country set their hands on the twenty-first day of June in the year herein first above written, do join in the cession made by the said Treaty and agree to adhere to the terms thereof in consideration of the undertakings made therein.

In witness whereof Her Majesty's said Commissioner and the Chief and Headmen of the Indians have hereunto set their hands at Wapiscow Lake, on this fourteenth day of August, in the year herein first above written.

Signed by the parties thereto in the presence of the undersigned witnesses after the same had been read and explained to the Indians by Alexander Kennedy.	J. H. Ross, *Treaty Commissioner,* his Joseph x Kapusekonew, *Chief,* mark his Joseph x Ansey, *Headman,* mark his Wapoose x *Headman,* mark his Michael x Ansey, *Headman,* mark his Louisa x Beaver, *Headman,* mark

A. E. Snyder, *Insp. N.W.M.P.*,
Charles Riley Weaver,
J. B. Henri Giroux, *O.M.I.*, *P.M.*,
Murdoch Johnston,
C. Falher, *O.M.I.*,
Alex. Kennedy, *Interpreter*,
H. A. Conroy,
(Signature in Cree character).
John McLeod,
M. R. Johnston.